THE CAYENNE &
COCOA COMPANION

THE CAYENNE & COCOA COMPANION

100 RECIPES AND REMEDIES FOR NATURAL LIVING

SUZY SCHERR

The Countryman Press

An Imprint of W. W. Norton & Company
Independent Publishers Since 1923

This book is intended as a general information resource. It is not a substitute for professional advice and no recommendation in this book to eat, drink, or use anything is intended to treat any condition or substitute for any prescribed medication. Consult your healthcare provider before changing your diet to include significant amounts of cayenne pepper or cocoa, especially if you are diabetic or suffer from an autoimmune condition or any other health condition (and especially if you are taking any prescription drug), if you are pregnant or nursing, or if you have food or other allergies. Do the same before you offer any new foods, ingredients, or products to children.

Cayenne pepper may interact adversely with blood thinners, aspirin, antacids, ACE inhibitors, and other medications, and ingesting large quantities of cayenne may cause digestive irritation. If you are allergic to latex, bananas, kiwi, chestnuts, or avocado, you also may be allergic to cayenne pepper. Do not use cayenne pepper near your eyes, open cuts, or broken skin. Cocoa, also, may cause certain adverse reactions, including skin rash and digestive issues. Be sure to read the warnings that accompany some of the product recipes about when not to eat or use certain foods or products, what precautions to take, and when to seek medical care instead of or in addition to using any home remedy.

Any URLs displayed in this book link or refer to websites that existed as of press time. The publisher is not responsible for, and should not be deemed to endorse or recommend, any website other than its own or any content not created by it. The author, also, is not responsible for any third-party material.

For information about permission to reproduce selections from this book, write to Permissions, The Countryman Press, 500 Fifth Avenue, New York, NY 10110

For information about special discounts for bulk purchases, please contact W. W. Norton Special Sales at specialsales@wwnorton.com or 800-233-4830

Manufacturing by Versa Press
Production manager: Devon Zahn

Library of Congress Cataloging-in-Publication Data

Names: Scherr, Suzy, author.
Title: The cayenne & cocoa companion : 100 recipes and remedies for natural living / Suzy Scherr.
Other titles: Cayenne and cocoa companion
Description: New York, NY : The Countryman Press, a Division of W. W. Norton & Company, [2022] | Series: Countryman pantry | Includes index.
Identifiers: LCCN 2021047624 | ISBN 9781682686324 (paperback) | ISBN 9781682686331 (epub)
Subjects: LCSH: Cooking (Hot peppers) | Cooking (Cocoa) | Naturopathy. | LCGFT: Cookbooks.
Classification: LCC TX803.P46 A524 2005 | DDC 641.6/384–dc23/eng/20211018
LC record available at https://lccn.loc.gov/2021047624

The Countryman Press
www.countrymanpress.com

A division of W. W. Norton & Company, Inc.
500 Fifth Avenue, New York, NY 10110

www.wwnorton.com

10 9 8 7 6 5 4 3 2 1

For M and I, my sweet and spicy girls

CONTENTS

MAINS

DRESSINGS, DRIZZLES, SPREADS, AND SAUCES

BEAUTY SECRETS   203

AROUND THE HOME   231

INTRODUCTION

For as long as I can remember, I've loved cooking. Ask me why and my knee-jerk response is usually to say something like "I love to take care of people" or "It's how I express my creativity." And while those things are absolutely true—and in that order—I also love the unpredictability of it. The element of surprise.

Say, for example, I'm making toast with butter. It's something I've made a zillion times and even though I'm certain I know what it will taste like when it's done, it's never *exactly* the same as the last time I made it. Perhaps I'll toast the bread a bit longer and it will be browner, or I'll use more butter than the last time, or maybe I'll slice the bread just a little bit thicker. So, even when I'm cooking something unbelievably familiar—so familiar it's basically ingrained in me—it's also new. Every single time. And that's with just the simplest of ingredients! Yes, I'm nerding out over toast with butter. I'll cop to that. But it's a perfect example of how you never know what little sparks will fly when you're in the kitchen. If simple, straightforward ingredients that we *know* work together can bring surprises, then what about combining foods that seem like they just won't work and then discovering that they're pure magic? Pretty great.

Cayenne and cocoa. Spicy and sweet. (Actually, cocoa is not sweet at all, but we mostly associate it with sweet, don't we? Much more on this later.) Ostensibly divergent flavors that are not only great friends, but have quite a bit in common. From

their origins to their health benefits, cayenne and cocoa are a lot alike in what they can do for our bodies, our homes, and our palates.

In cooking, they're much more indispensable than you might think, as they're both great for adding complexity, depth, and a good bit of the unexpected in everything from drinks to desserts and all courses in between. And while the kitchen is where my love for these two mighty ingredients emanates, it doesn't end there.

Together and apart, cayenne and cocoa show up all over my everyday life (and sometimes all over my kitchen floor, too—it's a good thing I've written books about apple cider vinegar and baking soda for a boatload of natural cleaning solutions!). I'm busy, like you. I'm a mom and wife and a chef and an author. My life, much like the cayenne and cocoa on my kitchen floor, is colorful, messy, and far from glamorous. And, because I much prefer to focus on the joy (having long ago given up on the possibility of perfection), I'm forever in search of ingredients I can use to easily improve and maintain my family's health, quickly beautify our home, and magically make my skin glow, my hair shine, and maybe even fake a tan. Cayenne and cocoa can do all that and—to be honest—they help preserve my sanity.

Both ingredients can multitask like a . . . well, like a busy mom! Cayenne—antimicrobial, antifungal, anti-inflammatory, and an excellent stimulant—is great for skin and hair, for use in wellness products that contribute to looking and feeling good, and for keeping your home and yard in tip-top shape. It's full of vitamins, phytonutrients, metabolism-boosting properties, and pain-fighting chemicals. Plus, it can help with conditions ranging from high blood pressure and stomach ulcers (yes, really!) to back pain and psoriasis—and it may even help our bodies fight off certain cancers—although this research is still ongoing, so best to take that info with a grain of salt. (Spicy margaritas, anyone?)

Cocoa, meanwhile, has been credited with everything from reduced systemic inflammation, increased blood flow, lower blood pressure, and improved cholesterol and blood sugar levels. It's especially high in flavanols, which have potent antioxidant and anti-inflammatory effects and, as such, may lower the risk of heart attack and stroke. Research also suggests it may help prevent age-related brain degeneration, such as in Alzheimer's disease.

I use cocoa to boost my mood, support my immunity, craft with my kids, and scent my home. I use it as part of my daily skin- and hair-care regimen and have even been known to literally take a bath in it. What chocolate lover hasn't had *that* fantasy?

This book will walk you through many of the easy and accessible ways in which I use cayenne and cocoa nearly every single day to take care of myself and my family. Together, we'll use both to awaken our senses, enhance our homes, feel better, and turn our everyday cooking into something sweet, spicy, unexpected, and—yes—perhaps even a bit messy. Just like life.

PART I

GETTING STARTED WITH CAYENNE AND COCOA

MEET CAYENNE

What Is It?

The cayenne pepper is a thin, red chili pepper that grows 2 to 5 inches long. A native of South America, it belongs to the *capsicum annuum* family of plants and is a relative of jalapeños, bell peppers, and New Mexico chili peppers. Typically found in the spice aisle of the grocery store as a finely ground powder, cayenne is one of the main ingredients in Tabasco sauce, and is commonly used in a wide range of world cuisines, such as Mexican, Creole, Indian, Thai, Chinese, Korean, and more. Cayenne peppers are considered somewhat spicy, ranging from 30,000 to 50,000 Scoville heat units. (The Scoville Scale measures the pungency of chili peppers and is based on the concentration of capsaicinoids—the chemical that makes chili peppers spicy.)

A Brief History of Cayenne

Cayenne, while popular today, is not exactly a "hot" new thing (get it?). It is thought to have been a part of the human diet since about 7,500 BCE and is one of the oldest cultivated crops in the Americas. The word "cayenne" is thought to be a derivation of the word *kyynha*, which meant "capsicum" in the ancient Tupi language once spoken in Brazil, although over time cayenne peppers have also been known as Bird's Beak, Chilliepin, and Guinea Pepper. Originally grown in Central and South America, indigenous populations used cayenne as a food and as a medicine for ailments ranging from stomachaches, cramping, and gas to disorders of the circulatory system.

Despite its far-reaching history, chili peppers—cayenne among them—were completely unknown to most of the world until Christopher Columbus made his way to the New World in the 15th century. As the story goes, King Ferdinand and Queen Isabella of Spain ordered Columbus to bring back gold and black pepper. He found neither. But as he ate the dishes the natives served him, he experienced the heat that chili peppers produce and, apparently, thought to himself, "same same." Of course, black pepper and chili pepper are botanically unrelated (black pepper comes from a berry-producing bush), but Columbus brought some back to Ferdinand and Isabella with the suggestion that they be used as an inexpensive replacement for black pepper. They were sold.

Once chili peppers landed in Europe, they spread around the globe faster than anything ever had. Within just a few decades, Spanish and Portuguese explorers had taken chili peppers all over Europe and to Asia, where they could be found in shops and gardens for both medicinal and culinary uses. Today, cayenne is frequently found in Indian, Asian, Mexican, African, Middle Eastern, and South American cuisines, to name a few, illustrating one constant in global cuisine: People all over the world love spicy food.

Health Benefits

Spicy and eye-opening, there's good reason cayenne has had such a long history in traditional and alternative medicine—

it's a powerful superfood with a plentitude of health benefits! Antimicrobial, antifungal, and anti-inflammatory, cayenne is chock-full of a huge range of beneficial chemical compounds and nutrients, including potassium and magnesium, as well as vitamins A, E, C, B6, and K. Cayenne's real superpowers—not to mention its powerful heat—come from the presence of capsaicin, its active ingredient. Its benefits to the body include regulating blood pressure and heart rate, maintaining healthy blood flow, fighting infections, promoting weight loss, boosting the immune system, preventing blood clots, regulating body temperature, and alleviating pain.

Cayenne has been shown to aid digestion, including soothing upset stomachs and cramps, slowing intestinal gas, treating and preventing ulcers, and curing constipation. Cayenne stimulates the salivary glands, which in turn kickstarts the digestive process, as well as the flow of digestive enzymes, which allows the body to metabolize food and eliminate toxins.

Cayenne also has powerful pain-relieving properties when applied topically. Studies indicate that capsaicin reduces the amount of substance P, a chemical that carries pain messages to the brain from your body. With less substance P in your body, pain messages can no longer reach the brain, which therefore helps you feel better. This can be particularly helpful in treating such conditions as osteoarthritis and rheumatoid arthritis, fibromyalgia, painful skin conditions such as psoriasis, surgical-related pain, low back pain, and other muscular discomfort.

Cayenne is great for conditions of the heart and blood

vessels, as it is a stimulant that can increase blood flow. It helps to improve poor circulation, reverse excessive blood clotting, lower high cholesterol, and prevent heart disease. And some research suggests that capsaicin acts as a thermogenic chemical, which can produce heat to stimulate your metabolism and help you burn fat.

With hefty doses of beta carotene and antioxidants that support your immune system, cayenne is especially helpful in kicking colds and flu. And thanks to its circulation-boosting properties, it aids in breaking up and moving mucus out of the body.

Early research suggests capsaicin may have anti-tumor properties and could even play a role in the treatment of certain cancers including colon, prostate, and gastrointestinal cancers.

SPICY WARNING

Do not give cayenne to children younger than 2 years old. Capsaicin ointment may be used on the skin for older children, but do not use topical cayenne ointments for more than two days in a row for a child.

People who are allergic to latex, bananas, kiwi, chestnuts, and avocado (like me—boohoo) may also have an allergy to cayenne.

After using cayenne, wash your hands well and avoid touching your eyes.

Buying and Storing Cayenne

Finding cayenne is not at all difficult—it's readily available, dried and powdered, in just about any grocery store. And while there's nothing *wrong* with buying cayenne from the

grocery store or an online retailer, the one disadvantage is that it's hard to know how old those peppers are. Cayenne, like most spices, loses its vibrancy fairly quickly—within about 9 months, so if you're able to source it from a vendor that specializes in spices (better yet, one that grinds their own), you've got a great shot at getting a really fresh product. If you don't have access to a reliable spice merchant, that's OK. Here are a few things to keep in mind to ensure you're using the best cayenne you can: 1) If you can't remember how long you've had your jar of cayenne, it's definitely too old to use; 2) Taste it! If it's faded, flavorless, or otherwise blah, toss it; and 3) Remember that cayenne is spicy stuff, so a little goes a long way. Therefore, you can get away with buying it in small batches, thus turning it over quickly.

When we cook with cayenne, most of the time we're using it in powdered form, but that's not the only way to buy it. From fresh and dried-whole, to flakes and powder, you'll want to consider what you're making in order to determine which form of cayenne you'll need.

Whole, fresh cayenne peppers are fantastic in stir-fries, salsas, hot sauces, pickles, and cocktails.

Whole, dried cayenne peppers are great for infusing alcohol and sauces with heat and flavor. They can also be rehydrated and used in salsa, sauces, soups, and stews. If you have a spice grinder, you can make your own cayenne powder from whole peppers.

Cayenne pepper flakes are what most of us know as "crushed red pepper" or "red pepper flakes." It's that stuff in the shaker on the pizzeria counter. Use it to add a pop of heat to a finished dish, in dressings, sauces, or other dishes where the texture will work well.

Cayenne powder is what's called for most often in this book. It's the spiciest form of cayenne and easiest to use in cooking. If you're new to cooking with cayenne, start slowly with ⅛ to ¼ teaspoon for a recipe with multiple servings or a small pinch if cooking for one. You can always add more, but you can't take it away!

OOPS—I ADDED TOO MUCH CAYENNE! NOW WHAT?

The easiest way to turn down the heat on a dish that's too spicy is to add more liquid, vegetables, protein, or whatever makes sense with your recipe to lessen the ratio of the cayenne to everything else. Dairy is another great way to tone down spiciness. Add milk, sour cream, or even a dollop of plain yogurt for a cooling effect.

The best way to store your cayenne is to keep it away from light, heat, and air. Spices don't require refrigeration, and, in fact, your fridge's humidity can actually harm your cayenne, so keep it out of there. As long as you're storing your cayenne in a cabinet or drawer (away from your stove), there's no need to transfer it out of the jar you purchased it in, but if you're keeping it out in the open, I highly recommend storing it in some kind of opaque tin or dark bottle.

MEET COCOA

What Is It?

To understand cocoa powder, it's helpful to have a tiny bit of background on where chocolate comes from and how it's made. In simplest terms, chocolate originates with the cacao bean, which is found inside a cacao pod—a large, gourd-shaped fruit with 30 to 40 seeds within. It grows on the cacao tree, otherwise known in science-y circles as *Theobroma cacao L.*

Unsweetened chocolate (also known as chocolate liquor or baking chocolate) is made when cacao beans are dried, roasted, pressed, and ground to a smooth paste. That paste consists of two components: cocoa solids and cocoa butter. Cocoa solids give chocolate its color and flavor; cocoa butter is the fat that gives chocolate its velvety "mouthfeel" and melting capabilities. To make cocoa powder, unsweetened chocolate is pulverized and then pressed to remove most of the cocoa butter. What results is a superfine, intensely flavored powder.

A Very Brief History of Cocoa

What we know as cocoa today is a far cry from where it all started thousands of years ago in ancient Mesoamerica (present day Mexico), where the first cacao plants were found. There, thanks to a humid and tropical climate, wild cacao trees flourished, yielding fruit that sustained wildlife and eventually became a prevalent part of Latin American culture.

The Olmec, one of the earliest civilizations in Latin America, were the first to turn cacao into chocolate, which they drank during rituals and used as medicine. A few hundred years later, Mayans revered chocolate as the drink of the gods, mixing roasted and ground cacao seeds with chiles, water, and cornmeal into a drink called "xocolatl," meaning "bitter water." By the 1400s, the Aztecs had begun not only consuming cacao but also using the beans as currency. They believed, as the Mayans did, that the beans had magical, even divine, properties suitable for use in sacred rituals of birth, marriage, and death. They drank it as a beverage mixed with native vanilla and chile peppers (and sometimes honey).

In the next century, during an expedition to the Americas, famed explorer Hernán Cortéz is said to have been first introduced to cocoa by the Aztec ruler Montezuma, who welcomed the Spaniard with the highly prized beverage, having mistaken him for a reincarnated god. (Oops!) Fascinated by indigenous cocoa-drinking customs, the conquistador brought cacao seeds home to Spain and thus began the rapid rise in popularity of chocolate in Europe. Initially cocoa was known primarily as a beverage, believed to have nutritious, medicinal, and even aphrodisiac properties. But it remained largely a privilege of the rich until the invention of the steam engine made mass production possible in the late 18th century.

The modern era of chocolate-making began with the invention of a game-changing hydraulic press that removed most of the cocoa butter from processed cacao. What resulted was a cake that could be pulverized into a fine powder, now known as cocoa, that soon led to the creation of solid chocolate. In 1828, Dutch chemist Coenraad Van Houten treated cocoa powder with alkaline salts to cut the bitter taste, creating a product known as "Dutch cocoa." Further developments such as Rudolphe Lindt's conching machine, the chocolate bar, milk chocolate, and the filled bon-bon transformed chocolate into products that soon developed even more widespread appeal. From there, the chocolate and cocoa industry exploded in popularity and quickly spread around the world.

Today, more than 4.5 million tons of cocoa beans are consumed annually around the globe in everything from drinks to candy bars!

Health Benefits

Whether you enjoy it by the beverage or the brownie, there's great news when it comes to consuming cocoa. For one thing, unlike chocolate, which, while undeniably delicious, is definitely what we call a "sometimes food" in my house, cocoa is something we can enjoy liberally. Yes, chocolate contains some healthy properties, but it's high in fat and sugar. (*Mmmm . . . fat and sugar . . . drool.*) Cocoa powder, on the other hand, depending on the brand, is just about 10 calories per tablespoon. It contains around 1 gram of fat, just 3 grams of carbs, and 1 gram of protein. Plus, it's high in fiber (about 2 grams per tablespoon), which does a whole lot of good. It stimulates the body's digestive enzymes and helps with the absorption of nutrients, and improves digestive function, gut health, and bowel regularity. Fiber can also help with weight management as it keeps you feeling fuller for longer.

What's more, cocoa is loaded with some of the most powerful antioxidants out there (higher, even, than well-known antioxidant superstars such as green tea or red wine). Among the most beneficial of those antioxidants is a flavonol called epicatechin. Flavonols are compounds found in plants that fight inflammation and protect against cell damage caused by free radicals. They support healthy blood flow, which is essential for the proper functioning of the heart, brain, skin, eyes, liver, immune system, digestive system . . . basically all of the systems in our bodies. It's even important for our exercise performance and recovery. Flavanols keep cholesterol from gathering in our blood vessels by stimulating the release of nitric oxide, which dilates blood vessels and increases blood flow, lessening the risk of blood clots, high blood pressure, and clogged arteries. They also lower the risk of lung cancer, prostate cancer, asthma, and type 2 diabetes. Cocoa's antioxidant powers protect our cells from premature oxidation or destruction and can help keep us looking and feeling younger, too. They help neutralize the damaging effects of free radicals on the skin, boost the production of collagen, increase cellular healing, and counteract signs of aging.

Cocoa is also chock-full of minerals, including iron, manganese, magnesium, and zinc, which work together to help your body function and give your immune system a boost. Magnesium in particular is essential for energy metabolism and healthy psychological function, bones, and teeth. Some studies even suggest that magnesium is one of the reasons women crave chocolate before their periods. It turns out we may actually *need* it, because magnesium not only promotes relaxation and reduces anxiety, but has also shown to help relieve menstrual cramps.

And speaking of cocoa's impact on mood—aside from its taste, which immediately invokes joy—there's phenylethylamine or PEA present in cocoa, which is a relative of amphetamines and acts as a mood elevator and natural antidepressant. It's the chemical our brains release when we're in love (chocolates on Valentine's Day make *so much* sense, right?). And there are other feel-good compounds at play too, including serotonin, caffeine, endorphins, tryptophan, and anandamide—all of which have been shown to enhance mood and create feelings of euphoria. No wonder we love the stuff!

From Bean to Brownie: How Cacao Becomes Cocoa

To say cultivating cacao is difficult is quite an understatement. For starters, the cacao plant only produces fruit within the latitudes of the Tropic of Capricorn and the Tropic of Cancer— regions around the equator. The trees grow naturally in shady conditions such as dense forests or on cacao farms, where they're planted in tandem with banana, acacia, or other shade-giving plants that protect them from wind and too much sun. Once planted, cacao growers have to wait 5 to 10 years for the trees to reach maturity and produce their first fruit. And while cacao trees produce about 100 flowers, only 10 to 15 of those actually remain on the plant and mature into fruit—a huge golden-red or purple melon-shaped berry that sprouts directly from the side of the tree and typically contains 30 to 40 seeds.

Harvesting cacao beans is a multistep process. First, the beans are removed from the fruit and undergo a 5- to 6-day fermentation, which reduces their natural bitterness and helps develop their intoxicating aroma. Next, they're dried for 1 to 2 weeks, after which they're cleaned, graded, packed, and shipped.

Once the beans reach their final destination, they're roasted and shelled to obtain the cacao kernel. The kernels are then crushed into smaller bits (called nibs), which are roasted again and finally ground into a thick paste called chocolate liquor. Pure chocolate liquor (unsweetened chocolate) typically contains 53 to 55 percent cocoa butter. The rest is pure cocoa solids. Some chocolate liquor goes through a specific set of processing steps to become chocolate confections, but to produce cocoa powder, the cocoa butter and cocoa solids are separated in a process using 25 tons of pressure from a hydraulic press.

The fatty, yellow cocoa butter is then squeezed out (and later used in chocolates, cosmetics, and medicines), leaving behind cocoa solids, which are dried and pulverized into the cocoa powder that we know and love.

Using, Buying, and Storing Cocoa

For such a familiar pantry staple, buying cocoa powder can actually get pretty confusing. Aside from the fact that there are countless brands to choose from, within those brands there's lots of lingo. Sometimes a recipe will call for "unsweetened cocoa"; others just suggest using "cocoa powder"; and still others call for "natural cocoa." And then, of course, there's "Dutch-processed" or "Dutched cocoa." Beyond that, there's organic, fair trade, single origin, raw cacao. It's a lot! So, in an attempt to demystify the whole shebang, here are a few good rules of thumb to keep in mind when shopping for cocoa:

Natural cocoa powder, sometimes called "unsweetened cocoa powder" or "pure cocoa powder" is the most common cocoa powder on supermarket shelves and what's called for most often in recipes. "Natural" simply means that, after being separated from the cocoa butter and ground into a powder, no other processing has taken place. The flavor of natural cocoa powder is fruity, somewhat astringent, and bitter, and it's light brown in color. When buying natural cocoa powder, the only ingredient on the label should be cocoa—no alkali or "Dutch processing" on the label or in the ingredients.

When to use it: Any time a recipe is not specific about using natural or Dutch cocoa, use natural. Not only is natural cocoa powder a more intense chocolate flavor, it is also quite acidic, with a pH level between 5.3 and 5.8. This makes it a great addition to recipes that include baking soda, as the cocoa will trigger the chemical reaction that causes lift and lightness in baked goods. As a result, natural cocoa powder works especially well in brownies, cakes, and cookies.

Dutch-processed cocoa powder, sometimes labeled as "processed with alkali" or "alkalized cocoa powder," is made by treating cocoa beans with an alkali solution—a process developed by a Dutch chemist in the 1800s—which offsets the acidity and cuts some of the bitterness. The result is a cocoa that is darker in color than natural cocoa powder and more mildly flavored with deeper, more earthy notes. Weirdly, the darker the color, the milder the taste.

When to use it: Generally speaking, if a recipe calls for baking powder or doesn't have to go in the oven at all (think ice cream, sauce, truffles, custard, etc.), you can use Dutch-processed.

Black cocoa powder is super dark Dutched cocoa powder. Heavy, repeated processing is what gives it that almost-black color. It's what gives Oreos and the outside of a traditional ice cream sandwich that characteristically deep hue.

When to use it: If you're looking to create a very dark baked good or maybe a sauce (although not necessarily one that is deeply chocolatey in flavor), this product is your ticket. Just as with Dutch-processed powder, use it in recipes that call for baking powder as the leavening agent.

Cacao powder is similar to cocoa powder, but it's processed at such a low temperature that the finished product, which is not roasted, is considered "raw." Cacao is much more bitter than cocoa, and because of its minimal processing, it is suspected to retain more of its beneficial nutrients.

When to use it: Anywhere you'd use natural cocoa powder, with the caveat that the finished product will be much less sweet. For this reason, cacao powder works especially well in savory cooking.

Other Considerations

Flavor: Just as when buying a chocolate bar, the flavors of the many cocoa types vary by brand. Sure, all cocoa powder shares some characteristics, but its ultimate flavor depends on the type of cacao beans, where it was grown, and how it was processed. In general, cocoa powder higher in fat will also have more flavor. The best tasting cocoa powders tend to have about 20 percent fat. Cocoa labeling doesn't always tell the whole story, but to get close, check the nutrition label and select a product with at least 1 gram of fat per serving.

Price: A cocoa powder's price can sometimes reflect the quality of the beans used; better beans contain more fat, which, as we know, equals richer flavor. That said, inexpensive cocoa powders aren't necessarily inferior. There are definitely some expensive cocoa powders no better than those that are regular-priced, so don't let cost dictate too much in your quest to find your favorite cocoa powder.

Responsibly sourced cocoa: You may want to consider sustainability and ethical growing practices when shopping for cocoa powder. The cacao supply chain is extremely complex and challenged by a variety of issues spanning deforestation, child welfare, poverty, and access to education. Brands such as Guittard and Valrhona—with third-party certifications such as "fair trade," "rainforest alliance," and "organic" on their labels—are good places to start. But exploring these issues in-depth through organizations such as the World Cocoa Foundation (www.worldcocoafoundation.org), whose vision is a "thriving and sustainable cocoa sector, where farmers prosper, communities are empowered, and the planet is healthy" is a great way to become an informed consumer.

At the end of the day, deciding which cocoa powder is "best" is largely about personal taste. And the only way to figure out which brands and styles you like is to try them out. Tough homework, I know. But no matter which kind of cocoa powder you grab, always check the label to make sure it's 100% cocoa with no sugars, stabilizers, or anti-caking agents added.

How to Store It

Storing cocoa is pretty straightforward. Keep it in an airtight container in a cool dry place. Well-stored cocoa powder will keep for up to two years.

PART II

CLEVER WAYS TO USE CAYENNE AND COCOA AT HOME

DELICIOUS
RECIPES

Appetizers, Snacks, and Sips

BUFFALO WINGS ✍

When it comes to Buffalo wings—from brining to deep-frying to *double* frying—there are a whole bunch of "secret" recipes out there and even more opinions as to what makes the crispiest, fieriest, most crave-worthy wings around. I happen to love a messy plate of *real* Buffalo wings—deep-fried and tossed in a mixture of butter and hot sauce.

But I must confess to being a bit of a party pooper when it comes to frying wings at home. Maybe it's because I subscribe to the double-fry camp of wing perfectionism and know that 1) twice-fried wings guarantee crispy skin and succulent meat and 2) twice-fried wings are a holy pain in the you-know-what, not to mention a big fat mess. I leave that heavy lifting to the bars and pubs, where they have the commercial equipment to do wings right.

Instead, I use an easy oven method that results in tangy, crispy, perfectly respectable wings that I can have any time I want. I highly recommend making these with homemade hot sauce (page 116), but using a commercially produced, cayenne-based hot sauce, such as the iconic Frank's RedHot, is traditional and damn good. And don't forget to pat your wings dry—that's the secret to getting crispy skin!

Serves 6 to 8

Continued

BLUE CHEESE DIP

½ cup sour cream

¼ cup mayonnaise

3 tablespoons fresh
lemon juice

3 ounces (about ½ cup)
blue cheese, crumbled

Kosher salt and freshly
ground black pepper

WINGS

3 pounds chicken wings,
separated into wingettes
and drumettes (see note)

1 teaspoon vegetable oil

Kosher salt and freshly
ground black pepper

½ cup homemade hot
sauce (page 116) or a
store-bought sauce such
as Frank's RedHot

4 tablespoons butter, melted

¾ cup celery sticks,
for serving

1. To make the Blue Cheese Dip: In a bowl, stir together sour cream, mayonnaise, and lemon juice. Fold in blue cheese; season with salt and black pepper. Cover and refrigerate until ready to serve, up to one day ahead.

2. To make the Wings: Pat the wings dry with paper towels. In a large bowl, toss them with the vegetable oil and season with salt and black pepper. Spread the wings on a foil-lined baking sheet, leaving about an inch or so of space between each wing.

3. Arrange an oven rack 4 to 6 inches below the heating element and turn on the broiler. Broil the wings 10 to 12 minutes, until the tops are browned and crisp. Flip the wings and broil 10 to 12 minutes more, until the wings are well browned and crisp.

4. While the wings cook, combine the hot sauce and melted butter in a large bowl.

5. When the wings are finished cooking, add them to the bowl with the sauce and toss to coat. Return the wings to the baking sheet, shaking off excess sauce, and broil for 2 to 3 additional minutes until deeply browned on both sides, flipping once.

6. Serve wings with the extra sauce, Blue Cheese Dip, and celery sticks.

Note: Most grocery stores sell wings already separated. If not, ask your butcher to chop them up for you. But it's really easy to do this step yourself. Simply look for two joints—one that connects the wing tip to the forearm and another that connects the forearm to the upper arm—and cut right through them, pushing down hard with the heel of your knife.

ROASTED CAULIFLOWER WITH CATALAN-STYLE COCOA-ALMOND PICADA

This dish starts simply enough with roasted cauliflower. Crispy, nutty, and golden, this uncomplicated, humble stuff is perfectly delicious just as it is. But then along comes this busy little so-and-so called picada: a Spanish pesto-like paste of ground nuts, garlic, olive oil, fried bread, and a whole slew of other aromatics that can vary from cook to cook, but often includes deep, earthy cocoa or chocolate!

Picada is most typically used as a thickener and flavor enhancer for stews and braises; it's not really intended for use as a sauce or condiment, but if you've ever cooked something with a picada and tasted it before adding it to the dish, then you know perfectly well that it is *delicious*! Like, lick-the-spoon delicious.

So, yes, I break all the rules here and use it as something of a sauce to enliven, deepen, and generally add a bomb of flavor to simple roasted cauliflower. And while I make mine with a fully unorthodox food processor (I'm a rebel, I tell you!), I have included directions for using a traditional mortar and pestle. Either way, you'll love this dish.

Serves 4 to 6

1 large head cauliflower, trimmed and cut into bite-sized pieces

5 tablespoons extra virgin olive oil

Kosher salt

1 slice stale country white bread, cut into 1-inch cubes

¼ cup blanched almonds

2 garlic cloves, whole

¼ cup roughly chopped
  parsley

⅛ teaspoon ground
  cinnamon

1 teaspoon unsweetened
  cocoa powder

½ teaspoon saffron

1. Preheat the oven to 425°F.

2. Toss the cauliflower with 1 tablespoon olive oil on a sheet pan, season with salt, and arrange in a single, even layer. Roast for 25 to 30 minutes, until the cauliflower is nicely browned and tender.

3. To make the picada: In a small skillet, heat 2 tablespoons of olive oil over medium heat. Add the bread cubes and cook, tossing frequently, until golden. Transfer the cubes to a plate and set aside.

4. Add the almonds and garlic to the skillet and toast, stirring frequently, until golden and fragrant, 3 to 4 minutes. Set aside.

5. Transfer the bread to a food processor. Add the almonds, garlic cloves, 2 tablespoons olive oil, parsley, cocoa powder, cinnamon, and saffron. Process to a paste. Alternatively, use a mortar and pestle to pound the picada ingredients into a smooth paste.

6. Arrange the cauliflower on a large serving platter and scatter the picada over the top. Serve warm or at room temperature.

ROASTED ALMONDS WITH COCOA AND SEA SALT

I happen to believe that almonds in any form are a delicious treat. They're a great source of healthy fat, fiber, and vitamin E, so they're a nutritional powerhouse, too. Whole, slivered, raw, roasted, salty, spicy ... deal me in. But if I had to choose a favorite almond form, it would be these delicious, nutritious, and super fun cocoa-dusted beauts. The recipe is so simple, it's almost a joke; you'll spend all of five minutes making them and can be eating them in as few as 20. The result is a crunchy, just-sweet-enough blast of chocolatey delight that is more healthy than not—a very good thing, as they're absolutely addictive. So ... feel free to go nuts! (Get it?)

Makes about 1 cup

1 cup raw almonds

1½ teaspoons olive oil

2 tablespoons unsweetened cocoa powder

1½ tablespoons confectioners' sugar

⅛ teaspoon coarse sea salt

1. Preheat the oven to 350°F.

2. Arrange the almonds on a parchment-lined baking sheet and drizzle with olive oil. Toss to coat. Bake for 10 to 12 minutes, stirring occasionally, until toasted and fragrant.

3. Meanwhile, in a medium bowl, combine cocoa powder, confectioners' sugar, and salt, whisking to incorporate.

4. Once toasted, transfer the almonds to the bowl with the cocoa mixture and toss until evenly coated. Cool completely before storing in an airtight container.

Note: The best way to measure cocoa powder is to first stir it or to give the container a gentle shake to loosen it, then spoon the cocoa into your measuring cup. Use the straight side of a spatula or knife to level it off. Never scoop cocoa directly out of the container or pack it into a measuring cup.

COCOA-MATCHA POPCORN

Popcorn is probably not the first thing you think of when you hear the word "matcha." And I'm guessing chocolate isn't either. I get it. The idea of combining the two and then throwing popcorn into the mix seems odd, to say the least. But, what can I tell you? *It just works.* You see, matcha, the vibrantly colored, antioxidant-rich Japanese green tea powder lends an earthy, sort of grassy, slightly floral, bitter flavor. That, balanced against the deep, also earthy, rich flavor of cocoa is a beautiful intersection. And when you marry those two with freshly popped popcorn, what you end up with is a salty-sweet, earthy and green, dark and bittersweet, complex crunch that you'll reach for again and again. You might even say it's a *matcha* made in heaven. (You guys, I'm sorry.)

Serves 4

2 tablespoons granulated sugar

2 teaspoons unsweetened cocoa powder

2 teaspoons matcha powder

1 teaspoon fine sea salt

9 to 10 cups freshly popped popcorn

2 tablespoons butter or coconut oil, melted

1. Combine sugar, cocoa powder, matcha powder, and salt in a small bowl. Mix well.

2. Add popcorn to a large bowl or spread on a large baking sheet. Drizzle the melted butter over the popcorn and toss to coat evenly. Sprinkle the cocoa mixture over the popcorn and toss again until well combined.

SPICY CHEESE CRISPS 🌶

These addictive little Cheddar crackers—buttery, savory, and spiced with cayenne—are just the thing to have along with a glass of wine. And, from the looks of my playroom rug last weekend, they are also just the thing to have while watching Saturday morning cartoons. (As it turns out, when you are 7 and 9 and you start watching TV at 6:45 a.m., you're ready for cheese crackers by 9 a.m.) Thankfully, the dough is dead-easy to make and comes together quickly. In fact, I think it probably takes longer to vacuum the crumbs in my playroom than it does to mix the dough. Unbaked dough can be stashed in the freezer so it's on hand for whenever you need it—no need to defrost; just slice with a sharp knife and bake.

Makes about 3 dozen

1 cup all-purpose flour

¾ teaspoon kosher salt

¼ to ½ teaspoon cayenne pepper, or to taste

8 ounces grated Cheddar cheese

½ cup softened butter

1. In a medium bowl, whisk together the flour, salt, and cayenne pepper. Add the Cheddar and softened butter and, using your hands, mix the ingredients until a soft dough forms.

2. Transfer the dough to a sheet of waxed paper or parchment and shape it into a 12-inch log. Wrap tightly and refrigerate for at least 1 hour and up to 1 week.

3. Position a rack in the center of the oven and preheat to 400°F. Line two baking sheets with parchment paper.

4. Slice the log of dough into ¼-inch-thick rounds; arrange 1 inch apart on baking sheets. Bake until the crackers are very lightly browned, 16 to 18 minutes. Cool completely on a wire rack.

SMOKY PUMPKIN SOUP 🌶

Creamy, smoky, earthy, and spicy...this vaguely Mexican-inspired soup is both comforting and—dare I say—*exciting*! That may seem a surprising descriptor for something as homey as pumpkin soup, but you'll see what I mean as soon as you try it. Smoky chipotle adds complexity and heat, which gets cranked up a bit more from the addition of cayenne; cumin adds earthiness; and a welcome hit of acidity comes from a generous squeeze of fresh lime juice. It's a winner, for sure.

I suggest using canned pumpkin, which makes this recipe quick enough to pull off on a weeknight, but you can most certainly use fresh pumpkin if you have it; about 2 pounds will yield the 2 cups of puree the recipe calls for. You can also sub in pretty much any other winter squash for the pumpkin—butternut, kabocha, or even sweet potato would work just fine. This soup freezes beautifully, so doubling it is a great idea. You can thaw it in the fridge overnight or, if you're like me and discover 20 minutes before dinnertime that you've forgotten to pull the soup out of the freezer, you can pop the frozen soup right into a saucepan and reheat it over medium-low heat. Crisis averted. *Whew*. If the soup separates, just puree it again until smooth.

Serves 4 to 6

Continued

2 tablespoons extra virgin olive oil

1 medium yellow onion, chopped

3 garlic cloves, chopped

1 teaspoon ground cumin

¼ teaspoon cayenne pepper

1 chipotle pepper (canned in adobo), chopped

2 teaspoons kosher salt, plus more to taste

Two 15-ounce cans canned pureed pumpkin

4 cups chicken or vegetable stock

1 teaspoon dried oregano

2 tablespoons lime juice

OPTIONAL GARNISHES

Mexican crema, sour cream, or crème fraîche

Toasted pumpkin seeds

Salsa

Fresh cilantro

Crushed tortilla chips

Chocolate shavings

1. In a large saucepan, heat the olive oil over medium-high heat. Add the onion and cook it until softened and fragrant, 3 to 4 minutes.

2. Stir in the garlic, spices, chipotle, and salt and cook 1 minute more.

3. Add the pumpkin, stock, and oregano then reduce the heat and simmer for 20 minutes, partially covered.

4. Puree the soup, using an immersion blender or in batches via a blender. Process until smooth.

5. Stir in the lime juice and taste to adjust seasonings. Ladle into bowls and serve with desired garnishes.

COCOA AND CAYENNE SPICED SNACK MIX

We take the business of snacking very seriously in our house. I, for one, come by it naturally. My dad was the indisputable King of Snacks—from cheese crackers to peanut butter–filled pretzels, the guy had something crunchy for every occasion, but also for no occasion at all. And because many of us end up marrying some version of our parents (before we full-on turn *into* our parents), I—naturally—married the Duke of Snacks, who has a deep and long-lasting affection for Chex Mix. I can't disagree. Chex Mix is hard to resist. Crunchy, salty, and deeply savory, it has a lot to offer. And, while it comes conveniently premade and bagged, store-bought snack mix can't hold a candle to the homemade stuff. Traditional Chex Mix, made with butter, Worcestershire sauce, a handful of seasonings, cereal, pretzels, and nuts is totally delicious. But I do believe that there's room to play around and a simple formula for making a great snack mix—such as the crunchy, spicy, sweet, and salty combo below—is easy to follow. It goes like this:

Pretzels (1 to 3 cups; any shape you like, with larger ones broken into bite-sized pieces)

+ Cereal (5 to 8 cups; up to four types, but nothing sweet. I like Chex, Crispix, and Cheerios best)

+ Nuts (1 to 3 cups; really anything goes here from peanuts to fancy mixed nuts)

Continued

+ Something *fun* and surprising (such as the sweet and salty cocoa/cayenne seasoning here; other ideas: coconut chips, dried fruit, sesame sticks, popcorn, wasabi peas)

+ Coat with sauce (½ cup melted butter, olive oil, or melted coconut oil mixed with seasonings of your choice: spices, Parmesan, soy sauce, honey . . .)

× Toast until crispy (30 to 45 minutes at 275°F is usually about right)

= Irresistible, snackable, packable, party-worthy munch!

Makes about 12 cups (never enough)

2 cups nuts of your choice
(or combination)

5 cups Chex cereal of your
choice (or combination)

2 cups mini pretzels or
mini pretzel sticks

2 cups bagel chips, broken
into smaller pieces

½ cup unsalted butter,
extra virgin olive
oil, or coconut oil

½ cup packed dark
brown sugar

1 teaspoon ground cinnamon

1 tablespoon unsweetened
cocoa powder

1 tablespoon kosher salt

½ to 1 teaspoon
cayenne pepper

1. Preheat the oven to 275°F. Line two baking sheets with parchment paper or silicone baking mats. Set aside.

2. Combine the dry snacks in a large mixing bowl. Set aside.

3. Combine the remaining ingredients in a medium saucepan set over medium heat. Stir until the butter and sugar have

melted. Pour over the dry ingredients and carefully stir to coat.

4. Divide the mixture evenly between the two baking sheets, spreading in an even layer, and bake for 45 minutes to an hour, stirring every 15 minutes, until toasted. Remove from the oven and allow to cool completely on the baking sheets.

5. Store in an airtight container at room temperature for 2 to 3 weeks.

CROSTINI WITH GOAT CHEESE AND COCOA NIBS 🌰

Meet cocoa nibs (or cacao nibs, as they're sometimes called), the coarsely ground bits of hulled cocoa beans that hardcore chocolate lovers' dreams are made of. They're crunchy, intense, full of nutrients, and deeply roasty-toasty-chocolatey in flavor. They're unsweetened and fairly bitter, lending themselves to both sweet and savory applications.

I love them on salads, in cookies, or even sprinkled on toast with peanut butter. But one of my favorite ways to use cocoa nibs is in this recipe, where I think they really show off their magic.

The idea here is inspired by an old-school cheese ball— remember those? Hulking mounds of blended cheeses, formed into a ball, then rolled in nuts and served with crackers. This is kind of a refined, more interesting version of that, where the tart creaminess of goat cheese plays off the deep nutty flavor of the nibs. Chèvre is rolled in a mixture of crushed cocoa nibs and a bit of Aleppo pepper for a touch of fruity heat, then sliced into rounds and served with a drizzle of honey. It's an easy appetizer or hors d'oeuvre that is always a hit with guests— with nary a shag carpet nor savory Jell-O mold in sight!

Makes about 24 pieces

One 8-ounce baguette, sliced into ¼-inch-thick rounds

1 tablespoon extra virgin olive oil, or more as needed

½ teaspoon kosher salt or flaky sea salt, plus more for seasoning the crostini

1 cup cocoa nibs

½ teaspoon Aleppo pepper flakes

One 8-ounce log mild chèvre-style goat cheese

¼ teaspoon honey (optional)

1. Preheat the oven to 400°F. Place the baguette slices on a baking sheet. Lightly brush each slice with the olive oil. Sprinkle with salt and bake until lightly toasted and crisp, about 8 minutes. Remove from the oven and allow to cool.

2. In a small bowl, combine the cocoa nibs, pepper flakes, and salt. Spread the cocoa nib mixture in a single layer on a sheet of foil. Roll the log of goat cheese in the mixture, pressing gently so the nibs stick.

3. To serve, carefully cut slices of the goat cheese about ¼ inch thick using a thin, sharp knife or—even better—a piece of unflavored dental floss. Really! It's one of the best ways to get nice, clean slices. Top each piece of toasted baguette with a round of crusted goat cheese and a drizzle of honey, if using.

Note: If you can't find Aleppo pepper, you can easily sub ancho chile powder or even crushed red pepper. The dish is also still very good with the hot pepper omitted entirely.

SWEET AND SPICY CANDIED BACON

Not long ago we lived through a time I like to call "The Age of Bacon Gone Mad," wherein bacon seemed to show up just about everywhere, including in places where it simply did not belong. It appeared in desserts: bacon in ice cream, cupcakes, chocolate bars, caramels, brownies. And while I get the whole salty/sweet, chewy/creamy, bright/smoky, yin/yang of it all, bacon-flavored vodka, air freshener, and toothpaste took it too far for me.

That said, there is one standout that emerged from the bacon-everywhere phenomenon: candied bacon. It's one of the few showstoppers that I can point to from an otherwise shameful period. It's been a hit in my house and, over time, I've played around with it a bit, varying the sweetener (coarse sugar, maple syrup, honey, etc.) and adding other flavors (chili powder, cinnamon, rosemary, etc.).

The beauty of this version is the extra layer of complexity that comes with the bright heat of cayenne. What results is a salty, sweet, and spicy treat that is pure magic crumbled on a salad, tucked into a sandwich, served as a garnish in a Bloody Mary, or displayed as a guest star on a brunch buffet. And the best part is that the only thing standing between you and delicious sweet and spicy candied bacon is about 30 minutes in the oven.

Serves 4 to 6

1 pound bacon (not thick cut) ¼ cup light brown sugar

¼ to ½ teaspoon cayenne
pepper, or to taste

1. Preheat the oven to 325°F.

2. Put bacon slices in a bowl, season them with the cayenne, and toss with the brown sugar.

3. Line a baking sheet with parchment or foil and arrange the bacon slices in a single layer on top. Sprinkle any remaining sugar from the bowl over the bacon. Top with another layer of parchment or foil and top that with a second baking sheet.

4. Place the tray in the center of the oven and bake for 20 to 30 minutes, until it is golden brown and crispy. Transfer the bacon (using tongs, please! It's molten sugar!!) to a serving platter or individual plates, where it will further crisp as it begins to cool.

COCOA BLUEBERRY SMOOTHIE 🍫

For the longest time, I wasn't much of a smoothie-for-breakfast kind of person. I liked them OK, but never found them satisfying enough to call a meal. Turns out, I was making them wrong! Sure, a fruit-heavy smoothie blended with milk or yogurt is creamy and refreshing. But once I figured out how to up the fiber and healthy fat quotient, I was in power-smoothie business. Now I make smoothies for breakfast quite often, always adding at least one special ingredient to keep things fun.

This cocoa and blueberry smoothie is loaded with antioxidants from both the blueberries and the cocoa, protein and healthy fat from nut butter and milk, and a dose of fiber and iron from the greens. The bananas add decadent creaminess and plenty of natural sweetness, although I sometimes try to keep my breakfast just a bit lower in sugar and have used 1 cup frozen riced cauliflower in place of the bananas with surprisingly excellent results!

Serves 2

2 small bananas, frozen

1 cup frozen blueberries

⅔ cup fresh kale or spinach leaves

4 to 6 Medjool dates

2 tablespoons almond butter (or nut butter of choice)

2 tablespoons unsweetened cocoa (or cacao) powder

2 cups milk (plant-based or cow's milk)

Optional add-ins: protein powder, collagen powder, maca powder, chia seeds, ground flaxseeds

Place all ingredients in a high-speed blender and blend for 1 minute until completely smooth.

CLASSIC BLOODY MARY 🌶

When my husband and I were dating, one of the nauseatingly cute discoveries we made early on was that we both had the same go-to drink order on an airplane: Bloody Mary mix. We agreed, "It's a snack *and* a drink in one." (I know, canned beverage bonding is *super* romantic—clearly we were destined to be together.) But it isn't just the satisfying, savory heft of a Bloody Mary that makes it a classic brunch (or flight) staple. There's the lingering, gentle burn from cayenne (or hot sauce) that really makes a Bloody Mary sing, and there's the irresistibly tangy base of tomato juice, lemon, and bracing horseradish. Plus, of course, that hit of vodka. All of which sets it apart from the rest of a brunch spread, often quite sweet with pancakes and waffles and syrup. It provides just enough heat to keep things interesting without overwhelming the rest of the cocktail. And because Bloody Marys are quite versatile, they can easily be made by the glass or pitcher and serve as a canvas for all manner of fun garnishes. They're perfect for entertaining. This version is fairly textbook, with plenty of tomato flavor and zing from cayenne. I do, however, offer a few fun ideas for garnishes and variations at the end, because . . . why not?

Serves 8

Continued

48 ounces tomato or vegetable juice (such as V8)

½ cup fresh lemon juice

1 tablespoon Worcestershire sauce

1 tablespoon hot sauce, such as Tabasco

2 teaspoons prepared horseradish

1 teaspoon celery seed

½ teaspoon freshly ground black pepper

16 ounces vodka

Celery stalks and lemon wedges, to serve

In a large pitcher, combine all the ingredients except the vodka. Stir well. Add the vodka and chill until ready to serve. Serve in tall glasses over ice with a stick of celery and wedge of lemon.

MAKE IT YOUR OWN

Garnishing a Bloody Mary is probably the most fun part of this cocktail. From the classic celery and lemon mentioned above to the less orthodox pickled shrimp and beef jerky, here are a few of my favorites:

Olives
Pickles (all kinds—onions, okra, green beans, asparagus, jalapeño)
Radishes
Fresh herb sprigs
Celery sticks
Lemon or lime wedges
A sprinkle of Old Bay seasoning
Flavored salts

Varying the booze in a Bloody Mary is another fun way to switch things up. Give one of these twists a try:

Bloody Maria: Use tequila or mezcal instead of vodka.
Bloody Caesar: Use clam juice with tomato juice or use Clamato in place of tomato juice.
Ruddy Mary: Use gin instead of vodka.
Virgin Mary: No booze instead of vodka.

RED WINE HOT COCOA

Yes, this is a recipe for hot cocoa with red wine *in* it, a surprisingly delicious combination. If you're feeling intrigued but skeptical, I was too when I first heard about this marriage of warming winter drinks. It turns out that the idea (which I, regretfully, did not invent—it has been making its way around the internet for a few years now) is genius. But why? It's not because of simple math. Sure, hot cocoa + good, mulled wine = good. But when it comes to combining two of life's greatest pleasures, some pairings work while others can be a disaster.

When cooking with wine, I usually recommend you use something you'd want to drink and often suggest not going overboard with varietal; in this instance, however, it's fairly key to the outcome. You're going to want to grab a bold and fruity wine, such as a merlot or zinfandel. They're both food-friendly with softer tannins and big, juicy fruit that can stand up to the intensity of the chocolate without creating a too-bitter finish that would come from a drier red. In nerd-speak, it has a lot to do with the polyphenols—remember those superstar antioxidant and anti-inflammatory properties in cocoa we've talked so much about? They're in red wine, too. The interesting thing about polyphenols in both wine and chocolate is that they aren't *just* good for you—they also affect flavor. The more polyphenols, the more bitter the taste. Zinfandel and merlot have just enough polyphenol concentration to complement the cocoa and dark chocolate in this drink without any harsh or bitter notes. In other words, hot cocoa + juicy red wine = creamy, dreamy chocolate bliss.

Continued

Makes 1 serving

3 tablespoons semisweet
or bittersweet
chocolate chips

1 tablespoon packed
brown sugar

2 teaspoons unsweetened
cocoa powder

A pinch of kosher salt

1 cup milk (full-fat
cow's milk, coconut
milk, or nut milk)

½ cup fruity red wine

OPTIONAL GARNISHES

Additional cocoa powder

Marshmallows

Cinnamon stick

1. Whisk the chocolate chips, brown sugar, cocoa, and salt together in a small saucepan.

2. Add the milk and bring the mixture to a low simmer over medium-low heat, whisking often until the chocolate is melted, about 2 minutes.

3. Add the wine and stir to combine.

4. Ladle the hot chocolate into a mug and garnish with a dusting of cocoa powder, marshmallows, or a cinnamon stick, if desired.

CHOCOLATE LIQUEUR

I always kind of liked the idea of chocolate liqueur and bought it a few times, but usually found it to be cloyingly sweet with an artificial taste. Because manufactures of beer, wine, and spirits don't have to list ingredients on their labels, who knows what kinds of chemicals go into those bottles? Still, I imagined boozy milkshakes, sweet martinis, chocolate-spiked coffee, chocolate liqueur–topped ice cream, and my favorite little rocks glass with a shot of decadent chocolate liqueur over ice. So rather than sulk about it, I decided to make my own (with all real ingredients, mind you), and—let me tell you—it couldn't be easier. If you get up right now and make this recipe, you can be drinking the most delicious chocolate liqueur as soon as it cools down! Although it really is delicious right away, the intensity of the vodka will mellow over time, so it gets better as it sits. The liqueur keeps for quite a long while in the fridge, which is probably irrelevant if you're at all like me and can't stop finding ways to use it.

Makes about 1 quart

¼ cup unsweetened natural cocoa powder

1 cup boiling water

1 cup granulated sugar

1 cup water

1 cup vodka

1. In a medium bowl, combine the cocoa powder and boiling water, stirring to dissolve the cocoa. Set aside.

2. In a small saucepan, combine the sugar and water and bring to a simmer over medium heat, stirring until the sugar has dissolved. Stir the sugar syrup into the cocoa mixture and add the vodka. Strain through a fine-mesh sieve into a container with a lid.

3. Refrigerate overnight.

COCOA AND CAYENNE BITTERS

If you're looking to step up your home mixology game—or even just looking for ways to make that glass of plain seltzer a bit more interesting—bitters are an absolute must. Essentially flavor extracts made from herbs, roots, spices, flowers, nuts, and other ingredients, I tend to think of bitters as more or less seasonings for drinks—kind of like the salt and pepper of the beverage world. We have a fairly extensive collection of bitters in our house that my husband has picked up over the years (he likes a few dashes added to his seltzer) in flavors ranging from orange to mint to whisky barrel and clove. While bitters are complex and intense, they're actually quite easy to make, if somewhat of an exercise in patience. The whole process takes a few weeks, so the most difficult part of the undertaking is the waiting. Here, a handful of warm spices come together with cocoa nibs and cayenne in a wakeup call for your palate. These bitters work beautifully in cocktails calling for dark spirits such as rum, tequila, and whisky. I especially love them in an old fashioned, which I make by combining a teaspoon of sugar, several dashes of bitters, and 2 ounces of whisky in a rocks glass with ice and a twist of orange.

Makes about 12 ounces

1½ cups vodka or high-proof grain alcohol

1 whole clove

2 cinnamon sticks, broken in half

2 tablespoons cocoa nibs

1 dried ancho chile, roughly chopped

2 teaspoons red pepper flakes or cayenne pepper

1. Combine the vodka, clove, cinnamon sticks, and cacao nibs in a glass jar. Seal and shake, then let steep at room temperature, away from direct sunlight, for 7 days.

2. After 7 days, add the ancho chile and cayenne or crushed red pepper. Steep for another 2 to 3 days.

3. Strain through a cheesecloth-lined fine-mesh sieve into a jar or bottle. Store at room temperature for up to a year.

TRULY SPICED CIDER, WITH OR WITHOUT BOOZE 🌶

Nothing screams fall quite like a steaming mug of mulled cider. It's comforting, naturally sweet, subtly (or in this case, not-so-subtly) spiced, and insanely delicious. It's the perfect welcoming drink to make for a crowd and is festive enough to serve at a holiday gathering. I've kicked things up a notch with a nice hit of cayenne, which results in a sweet-and-spicy punch that takes this cool weather standby to new territory. Otherwise, however, this cozy recipe is very straightforward: You'll steep apple cider with spices and a bit of orange zest (in the slow cooker, if you like—3 to 4 hours on LOW), then strain it into glasses. A splash of good bourbon, rum, or brandy is not mandatory but is certainly welcomed!

Serves 6

1 quart fresh apple cider or unfiltered apple juice

4 whole black peppercorns

1 cinnamon stick, broken in half

One 1½-inch piece fresh ginger, sliced thin

1 teaspoon whole dried cloves

½ teaspoon cayenne pepper

1 medium orange

Bourbon, rum, or brandy (optional)

OPTIONAL GARNISHES

Cinnamon stick

Apple slices

Orange slices

1. Place the apple cider and spices to a saucepan. Using a vegetable peeler or sharp paring knife, peel away a couple of thick strips of peel from the orange and add them to the pan. Bring the cider mixture to a boil, lower the heat, and simmer for 5 minutes.

2. Carefully strain the cider into mugs. Add 2 to 3 tablespoons of spirits, if using, to each mug. Serve hot, garnished as desired, with cinnamon sticks, apple slices, and/or orange wheels.

SPICY POMEGRANATE ICE CUBES 🌶

We can all agree that ice is an important component of drink making. *Because it's... um, cold?* That's right, ice makes drinks cold. *And cold drinks are, well, sometimes better than lukewarm ones?* Correct! Perhaps that's about as much thought as you've ever put into the ice that goes into your drinks. But maybe you've also considered the shape of your ice. Some drinks work especially well with crushed ice; others demand a large spherical shape, which melts slowly and won't water down that high-priced Scotch you sprung for. But have you considered flavoring your ice? If not, you should! Flavored ice cubes are such a fantastic way to zhuzh up a cold drink and give it a little pizzazz.

You can puree seasonal fruit or use juice (think berries, stone fruit, or watermelon in the summer; citrus in the winter) to make ice cubes. They freeze just as well as water and add a pop of color and flavor to cocktails, seltzer, or water. Fresh herbs and edible flower petals (organic, unsprayed only, please!) are beautiful additions to ice cubes that will give your drinks both subtle flavor and a beautiful garnish.

These spicy pomegranate ice cubes are not only a gorgeous color, but they also slowly infuse drinks with sweet-tart flavor and a hit of heat as they melt. They're especially pretty added to a clear drink where their color really shines, but I also love them in lemonade, unsweetened iced tea, and margaritas, sangria, and gimlets.

Makes 1 to 2 dozen ice cubes, depending on ice cube size and shape

1¼ cups pomegranate juice

¼ cup water

¼ to ½ teaspoon cayenne pepper, or to taste

1. Combine juice, water, and cayenne in a small bowl or liquid measuring cup. Mix well.

2. Pour the juice mixture into 1 or 2 ice cube trays and freeze 3 to 4 hours until solid.

Mains

WEEKNIGHT CHICKEN MOLE

I would be remiss if I didn't include a recipe for mole in a book about chiles and cocoa! Mole is *sort of* a catch-all term for sauce in Mexican cuisine. But the mole most of us neophytes know best is the deep, dark chocolate–spiked version known as mole poblano. While I have traveled a bit in Mexico, I must admit that my first introduction to mole was in Laura Esquivel's beautiful novel, *Like Water for Chocolate*, where each chapter begins with a recipe. Tita's Turkey Mole with Almonds and Sesame Seeds (chapter four, if you're wondering) stopped me in my tracks. It was the first time I'd seen chocolate used in a savory dish and my mind was blown; I had to make it instantly. Built on layers upon layers of flavor (thanks to an ingredient list about 20 items long), the finished product was incredibly delicious, but quite literally an all-day affair. And, while I'm all for a good dive-in-head-first cooking project, I get even more excited about taking the essence of a dish like that and turning it into more of a no-brainer. As such, I bring you this pared-down version of chicken with mole sauce. Is it authentic? No. But it definitely delivers as far as depth and richness go, with a delicious blend of chile peppers, nuts, raisins, cocoa, and, of course, love. The recipe makes more than you'll reasonably eat in one sitting, but you can easily freeze the leftovers.

Serves 4

2 to 3 pounds bone-in, skin-on chicken thighs

2 teaspoons extra virgin olive oil, plus more for browning the chicken

Kosher salt and freshly ground black pepper

Toasted sesame seeds, for garnish

MOLE SAUCE

½ medium yellow onion, diced

1 clove garlic

2 teaspoons chili powder, preferably ancho chile

½ teaspoon kosher salt

¼ teaspoon ground cinnamon

⅛ teaspoon ground cloves

¼ teaspoon freshly ground black pepper

1 tablespoon tomato paste

1 tablespoon unsweetened natural cocoa powder

2 tablespoons raisins

1 tablespoon toasted sesame seeds

¾ cup tomato sauce or puree

2 to 3 cups water or chicken broth

2 tablespoons almond or peanut butter

1. Arrange a rack in the middle of the oven and heat to 400°F.

2. Drizzle the chicken thighs with olive oil and season well with salt and black pepper. Place the thighs skin-side down in a single layer in a large, cold, cast-iron skillet. Place the skillet over medium heat and cook for 14 to 15 minutes, until the skin is crispy and brown.

3. Meanwhile, make the mole sauce: In a small skillet, sauté the diced onion in olive oil until soft and translucent. Add the garlic and sauté another minute. Add the spices and cook, stirring, for about 30 seconds.

Continued

4. Transfer the onion and spice mixture to a blender or food processor. Add the tomato paste, cocoa, raisins, sesame seeds, tomato sauce, ½ cup water or broth, and almond butter and process until smooth. Set aside.

5. When the chicken is well browned, turn it and pour the mole sauce over the thighs. Transfer the skillet to the oven and roast until the chicken reaches an internal temperature of 165°F, about 15 minutes. Serve immediately, garnished with a sprinkling of toasted sesame seeds.

NASHVILLE HOT CHICKEN 🌶️

This recipe dates back to 1930s Nashville, when a relentless womanizer named Thornton Prince cheated on his girlfriend one time too many. Seeking a bit of revenge, she doused his beloved fried chicken in spicy sauce, hoping to make it inedible. To her great dismay, not only did Thornton love it, he shared it with his brothers, who loved it, too. And soon enough, Prince's Chicken Shack, the original home of Nashville's Hot Chicken, was born. Prince's is still around today, run by the original owner's great-niece, and they still make irresistible fried chicken with a major kick thanks to hot sauce and cayenne in the coating as well as a spicy sauce drizzled over the top. It's served with white bread and pickle slices to sop up some of the saucy goodness and help balance out the heat.

If you're lucky enough to find yourself in Music City, I highly recommend seeking out the real deal. It's pretty life changing. But if not, you can make a fantastic version at home. Admittedly, there are quite a few steps to this recipe, but it's neither difficult nor particularly time consuming and, most important, *It's. So. Worth. It.* I suggest using dark meat here, because I just think it tastes so much better than white meat and it's much less prone to dry out. Try it my way *just once* and see if you disagree. If you absolutely must use breasts (it's OK, you do you!), you'll likely find that you need to cook them a bit longer to reach an internal temperature of 165°F.

Serves 4

Continued

2 tablespoons cayenne
  pepper

2 tablespoons paprika

1 tablespoon garlic powder

1 tablespoon mustard
  powder

1 tablespoon freshly
  ground black pepper

1 tablespoon onion powder

4 bone-in, skin-on
  chicken thighs

4 chicken drumsticks

1 tablespoon kosher salt

2 cups buttermilk

2 tablespoons hot sauce (you
  can use the homemade
  hot sauce on page 116)

1 tablespoon light
  brown sugar

2 cups all-purpose flour

Sliced white bread and
  pickles, to serve (optional)

1. In a medium bowl, whisk together the cayenne pepper,
   paprika, garlic powder, mustard powder, black pepper,
   and onion powder. Set aside.

2. In a large bowl, place chicken and pat dry. Toss with
   5 tablespoons of the spice mix and the salt, taking care to
   fully coat the chicken pieces.

3. Cover and refrigerate for at least 30 minutes and up to
   24 hours.

4. In a medium bowl, combine the buttermilk and hot sauce.
   Stir to incorporate. Set aside.

5. Dredge each piece of chicken into the flour, shaking off any
   excess. Dip them into the buttermilk mixture, then back
   into the flour.

6. Fill a 6- to 8-quart pot halfway with oil and heat it to
   325°F. Working in batches, lower the chicken into the oil

and fry until crisp, 15 to 20 minutes. Transfer the fried chicken to a wire rack set over a baking sheet.

7. Carefully ladle ½ cup of the hot frying oil into a medium heatproof bowl and whisk in 2 tablespoons of the spice mix and the brown sugar. Baste the chicken with the spicy oil and serve immediately with sliced white bread and pickles, if desired.

COCOA MOLASSES TURKEY TENDERLOIN 🍫

Turkey tenderloin, so often overlooked, is a tidy little package of lean protein that will feed a family and can be on the table in under 30 minutes. Because the tenderloin—a thick strip of meat between the bird's breasts—doesn't get much of a work-out during a turkey's life, the meat is especially tender. It's also incredibly versatile, working well with just about any flavor profile and cooking method, so you can slather it, rub it, or marinate it with just about anything and then grill, roast, pan-fry, or stuff it for a quick and satisfying meal.

This recipe involves simply searing the cocoa-dusted meat in a skillet, then roasting it in the oven until tender and juicy. Meanwhile, you'll make a quick and flavorful sauce that you'll want to take a bath in. Trust me. Any leftover turkey is great on a sandwich the next day, smothered with some of that sweet-and-sour, spicy, and deep sauce. Just remember to keep an eye on the internal temperature, making sure not to overcook the turkey. It's done at 165°F, but you can pull it out of the oven when it hits 160°F or so because it'll keep cooking as it rests.

Serves 4

1 tablespoon olive oil

2 (1¾ to 2 pounds total) unseasoned turkey tenderloins

Kosher salt and freshly ground black pepper

1 tablespoon unsweetened natural cocoa powder

1 tablespoon Aleppo pepper (optional; may substitute sweet paprika)

Zest and juice of 1 navel orange

1 jalapeño pepper, seeds and membrane removed, sliced thin

1 teaspoon ground coriander

3 tablespoons molasses

2 tablespoons dark brown sugar

1 tablespoon red wine vinegar

½ cup water

2 bay leaves

1. Preheat the oven to 375°F.

2. Heat the oil in a large ovenproof skillet over medium-high heat. Season the turkey with salt and black pepper, sprinkle the cocoa powder and Aleppo pepper evenly over the meat, then brown well on all sides.

3. Transfer the pan to the oven and roast for about 20 minutes, until an instant-read thermometer registers 165°F. Allow the meat to rest for 5 minutes.

4. Meanwhile, combine the orange zest and juice, jalapeño, coriander, molasses, brown sugar, red wine vinegar, water, and bay leaves in a small saucepan. Cook over medium heat for about 5 minutes, stirring occasionally, until the sugar has dissolved and the liquid is slightly reduced. Set aside.

5. Slice the tenderloins crosswise into 1-inch pieces, spoon the sauce over the meat, and serve.

SMOKY ESPRESSO AND COCOA RUBBED STEAK

Here's an instance where cocoa powder adds that elusive kind of savory magic to a dish. Despite calling for a full tablespoon of cocoa in the rub, the steak doesn't end up tasting chocolatey. It's deep, rich, and complex, but if you didn't know there was cocoa in the recipe, I'm guessing you'd be hard pressed to call it out. It simply adds an element of *je ne sais quoi*! The cocoa, along with espresso powder and a touch of chipotle, brings a smoky depth to this crowd-pleasing flank steak. If you like, you can rub the steak ahead of time and let it rest in the refrigerator for several hours, or even overnight, to allow the flavors to really permeate the meat. And while I suggest you grill the flank if possible (it's SO good), you can certainly make a delicious steak under the broiler; the cooking time won't change.

Serves 6 to 8

1 tablespoon unsweetened natural cocoa powder

1 tablespoon finely ground espresso powder

½ teaspoon chipotle powder or smoked paprika

1 tablespoon kosher salt

1 teaspoon freshly ground black pepper

One 3-pound flank steak

1. Preheat a grill to medium.

2. Stir together cocoa, espresso powder, chipotle powder, salt, and black pepper in a small bowl.

3. Generously coat the steak on all sides with the cocoa rub. Place the steak on a preheated grill and cook for 6 to 7 minutes. Turn the steak over and cook for another 4 to 6 minutes for medium-rare.

4. Transfer the steak to a cutting board and let it rest for 5 to 7 minutes before slicing thinly across the grain.

OVEN-BAKED CINNAMON, GINGER, AND COCOA RUBBED BABY BACK RIBS

I am far from a BBQ expert. I'd never refer to myself as a pit boss or a grill master. I don't have a smoker or even a charcoal grill. I know a lot less about briquettes than I do about brisket. And yet, I know how to make some seriously kickass ribs. And here's the kicker—I do it without a grill. Rubbed with a mixture of warm spices, earthy cocoa, and fiery cayenne, these ribs cook slow and low in the oven until they're succulent, smoky-sweet, and savory. And by low and slow, I mean really low and really slow. Like, 275°F for more than 3 hours. Sure, they're time consuming, but the recipe is almost entirely hands-off and it's 100 percent worth the wait. If you want to earn some 'cueing street cred, tie on your "Hot Stuff Coming Through" apron and finish off these ribs on a preheated grill rather than following the last step below. Who's the pit boss now?!

Serves 4 to 6

⅓ cup unsweetened natural cocoa powder

¼ cup chili powder (such as ancho)

2 teaspoons smoked paprika

2 tablespoons onion powder

1 tablespoon garlic powder

1 tablespoon dried oregano

1 tablespoon dried mustard

2 teaspoons dried ginger

2 teaspoons ground cinnamon

1 teaspoon ground allspice

1 tablespoon kosher salt

2 teaspoons freshly ground black pepper

2 racks (about 3 pounds) baby back ribs

12-ounce can beer

¼ cup light brown sugar

1. Preheat the oven to 275°F.

2. Stir together cocoa, spices, herbs, salt, and black pepper in a small bowl.

3. Place ribs on a foil-lined baking sheet and coat with half of the rub, using a bit of firm pressure to help it adhere to the meat. Place the ribs in the oven and cook for about 2 hours, uncovered, until the fat has rendered and the meat begins to yield to a fork when pierced.

4. Remove the ribs from the oven and set them on top of two large overlapping pieces of foil that have been crimped together along their long edge. Pour the beer on top of the ribs, cover tightly with additional foil, and return to the oven to continue cooking for about an hour more, until it's fall-off-the-bone tender.

5. Meanwhile, add the brown sugar to the remaining rub and stir to combine. Remove the ribs from the oven and

Continued

increase the temperature to 400°F. Discard the liquid that's collected on the sheet pan, carefully rub the ribs with the brown sugar mixture, and return them to the oven for 10 to 15 minutes. When the brown sugar rub caramelizes and is just on the cusp of burning, pull the pan out of the oven. Serve immediately with plenty of napkins!

FRENCH-STYLE BEEF STEW 🍫

If you ask me, everyone should have a slam-dunk beef stew rec-ipe in their back pocket—something that warms you from the inside out, a hug in a bowl. This recipe is just that. Inspired by a traditional French stew from the Gascony region of France called *a daube*, which just means it's a stew cooked in wine, it's beefy, rich, and fragrant with Cognac, cocoa, and—yes—a whole lot of wine. Technically, it's a very simple recipe: The meat gets browned in a Dutch oven (or a daubiere, if you happen to have the French cooking vessel named after the stew) and then is slowly braised with vegetables, herbs, wine, Cognac, and—of course—cocoa, which adds richness and depth. You can abso-lutely serve this stew as-is with nothing more than a green salad and loaf of good country bread, but if you're anything like me and love a good carb-y base on which to ladle your stew, potatoes mashed with olive oil, buttered egg noodles, or even some soft polenta would all be most welcome here.

Serves 6 to 8

Continued

3 ounces slab bacon, cut into ½-inch dice

3½ pounds chuck beef, cut into 2-inch pieces

Kosher salt and freshly ground black pepper

2 tablespoons olive oil

10 cloves garlic, roughly chopped

3 medium carrots, cut into ½-inch pieces

2 parsnips, peeled and cut into ½-inch pieces

1 large yellow onion, cut into ½-inch pieces

⅓ cup armagnac, cognac, or another brandy

1 (750-milliliter) bottle light-bodied red wine, such as pinot noir

1 cup beef or chicken broth

1 bouquet garni (3 sprigs parsley, 3 sprigs thyme, 2 bay leaves, and 2 sprigs rosemary tied together in a piece of cheesecloth)

2 tablespoons unsweetened natural cocoa powder

1. Preheat the oven to 350°F.

2. In a Dutch oven over medium heat, add the bacon, and cook until the fat is rendered and the bacon is browned, 5 to 7 minutes. Using a slotted spoon, transfer the bacon to a large bowl; set aside.

3. Season the beef with salt and black pepper. Working in batches, brown the beef on all sides, resisting the urge to crowd the pan (you'll steam the meat instead of browning it. Gray meat. *Ew*.). Transfer the browned meat to the bowl with the bacon.

4. Add garlic, carrots, parsnips, and onion to the pot and cook, stirring occasionally, until just beginning to brown, 10 to 12 minutes.

5. Take the pot off the heat momentarily and add the brandy. Return the pot to the heat and cook, stirring and scraping up browned bits from the bottom of the pan until the liquid is reduced by half, 1 to 2 minutes. Return the beef and bacon to the pot, add the wine, broth, and bouquet garni and bring it to a boil.

6. When the mixture comes to a boil, cover the Dutch oven and place the stew in the oven to braise for 2 to 2½ hours, stirring once or twice, until the beef is very tender.

7. Remove the bouquet garni, stir in the cocoa powder, and season to taste with salt and black pepper. Serve.

LOUISIANA-INSPIRED JAMBALAYA 🌶

The first time my husband and I traveled to New Orleans, I dove deep into the internet and amassed quite a robust list of spots where we'd find the very best po boy, gumbo, Sazerac, pecan pie, beignet, and—of course—jambalaya. When it came to making a hotel reservation, I was not so lucky. Everywhere I tried was booked. *Hmm . . . there must be a convention in town*, I thought to myself.

I did eventually finagle a room in town at the very last minute, but it literally wasn't until we arrived in the French Quarter that we realized, *no*, there wasn't a convention in town. It was Mardi Gras! (Duh.) So, although we got to see all the incredible pageantry and the parades, the crowds meant we didn't make quite the dent on our eating agenda that we'd set out to.

That said, we did manage to enjoy a most memorable serving of jambalaya. Although it's far from authentic, I do make a version at home every now and again, and, let me tell you, I'm not half bad for a northerner! I've taken some liberties, but the basics of a good jambalaya are all there: rice loaded with meat, seafood, tomatoes, the holy trinity (onion, celery, and bell pepper), and plenty of cayenne pepper. It's warm, comforting, spicy, and takes me back to NOLA every time. (Sigh . . .)

Serves 4 to 6

Continued

1 teaspoon kosher salt, plus more as needed

1 teaspoon finely ground black pepper

½ teaspoon cayenne pepper

1¼ pounds boneless skinless chicken thighs, cut into 1½-inch pieces

2 tablespoons olive oil

½ pound andouille sausage, thinly sliced (may sub with kielbasa or another smoked sausage)

1 large yellow onion, finely chopped

2 ribs celery, finely chopped (about 1 cup)

2 green bell peppers, seeded and finely chopped

4 garlic cloves, minced

2 tablespoons tomato paste

One 14.5-ounce can diced tomatoes

3½ cups chicken stock

¼ teaspoon dried thyme

3 bay leaves

2 teaspoons Worcestershire sauce

1½ cups long grain white rice

1 pound medium shrimp, peeled and deveined

Thinly sliced green onions, for garnish (optional)

1. In a large bowl, combine the salt, black pepper, and cayenne. Add the chicken and toss to coat. Set aside.

2. Place the olive oil in a large heavy saucepan or Dutch oven over medium heat. Add the sausage and cook, stirring occasionally, until the fat has rendered and the sausage is browned, 5 to 7 minutes. Using a slotted spoon, transfer the sausage to a large bowl; set aside.

3. Add the chicken to the pot and cook, stirring occasionally, until it's browned and cooked through, about 8 minutes. Again, using a slotted spoon, transfer the chicken to the bowl with the sausage.

4. Add the onion, celery, and bell peppers to the pot and cook, stirring occasionally, until they're softened and just beginning to brown, 10 to 12 minutes.

5. Add the garlic and tomato paste and cook, stirring until fragrant, about 1 minute. Add the diced tomatoes with their juice, chicken stock, thyme, bay leaves, and Worcestershire sauce and bring the mixture to a boil over high heat. Reduce to a simmer.

6. Add the sausage and chicken along with the rice. Stir, then cover and cook for about 20 minutes, until the rice is tender.

7. Stir in the shrimp and cook until they are just done, 3 to 5 minutes more. Serve warm, garnished with green onions, if desired.

SHRIMP SALAD 🌶

Not to stir up controversy or anything, but I'm not a huge lobster fan. Oh, relax! It's not like I said puppies aren't cute! I just happen to prefer shrimp when it comes to seafood. And that sentiment holds true especially when it comes to any sort of seafood salad. Look, if you offered me a lobster roll right now, I'd eat it. I'm not an idiot! But I find that lobster is a bit mild for my taste—there's not much *there*, if you know what I mean. I'd get much more excited if you handed me a shrimp roll, stuffed with the bright, tangy, spicy salad below. It's a snap to make, really flavorful, and about as evocative of summer vacation as dishes get. The addition of both horseradish and cayenne pepper brings the shrimp to life, cuts the creaminess of the mayonnaise, and balances the natural sweetness of the shrimp. In a pinch, precooked, frozen shrimp will work in this recipe, but I highly recommend you steam fresh shrimp, as directed below. They'll be far more tender and much more flavorful. You can certainly scoop this salad onto a sandwich with lettuce and tomato on good bread or serve it on top of greens, but my favorite way to eat it is lobster roll–style, stuffed into buttered, griddled, top-split hot dog rolls. And, yes, I would like fries with that.

Serves 4 to 6

1 pound medium shrimp, wild-caught, if possible

2 celery stalks, finely chopped

¼ cup mayonnaise

3 tablespoons fresh lemon juice

1 tablespoon prepared horseradish

¼ teaspoon kosher salt

¼ teaspoon cayenne pepper, plus more to taste

A few dashes of homemade hot sauce (page 116) or store-bought

1 tablespoon chopped fresh parsley

1. Set a steamer basket over 1 to 2 cups of boiling water in a medium saucepan. Add the shrimp and steam until they're just cooked through, 4 to 5 minutes. Remove the shrimp from the steamer basket and allow them to cool completely in an ice bath.

2. Peel and devein the shrimp and chop roughly.

3. In a large bowl, stir together the celery, mayonnaise, lemon juice, horseradish, salt, cayenne, and hot sauce.

4. Add the shrimp and parsley, and toss until coated in the dressing. Taste to adjust seasonings, as desired.

BOUILLABAISSE 🌶

Bouillabaisse is a rich, fragrant stew that comes from Marseille in the Provence region of southern France. It traditionally contains several types of fish in an orange-hued broth, scented with an intoxicating blend of saffron, fennel, and orange zest. There are probably about as many versions of Bouillabaisse as there are cooks in Marseille—some heavy with tomato, others without; some made strictly with fin fish, others that include a variety of shellfish; some with thick broth, others with thin. But in all cases, the combination of saffron, fennel, and orange (absolute musts in a *true* Bouillabaisse) paired with fresh fish is a beautiful thing. My riff below is moderately tomatoey and includes as many or as few varieties of mild, white fish as you like and the optional addition of mussels.

All fish soups in southern France are traditionally served with sauce rouille, which I happen to think is the star of this show. Rouille is a creamy, spicy, aioli-like sauce that can be spooned over the top of a bowl of Bouillabaisse or smeared onto crusty bread, then dipped in the soup. It's a perfect illustration of how cayenne can add the right punch of flavor to a dish. Here, the spicy rouille plays beautifully against a delicate backdrop of soup. I've saved you the trouble of making your own mayonnaise for the sauce (even though it's very easy to do so, per my book *The Olive Oil & Sea Salt Companion*), but good-quality, store-bought mayonnaise will not compromise the deliciousness of the rouille—I promise.

Serves 6

¼ cup extra virgin olive oil

1 large yellow onion, diced

1 large red or yellow
bell pepper, diced

1 large fennel bulb, diced

¼ cup fennel fronds, plus
more for garnish

1 teaspoon saffron threads,
steeped in 1 tablespoon
hot water for 5 minutes

Pinch of cayenne pepper

4 cloves garlic, minced

1 cup dry white wine

2 tablespoons Pernod
(or another Pastis)

4 cups seafood stock

One 14.5-ounce can
diced tomatoes

1 tablespoon grated
orange zest

Kosher salt and freshly
ground black pepper

2 pounds mussels, scrubbed
and debearded (may
sub clams or use a
combination)

3 pounds white fish fillets
such as cod, striped
bass, grouper, and/
or red snapper, cut
into 2-inch pieces

¼ cup minced parsley,
for garnish

Sliced baguette, for serving

Rouille (page 103),
for serving

1. In a large pot or Dutch oven, heat the olive oil over medium
   heat. Add the onion, bell pepper, fennel, fennel fronds, saffron, and cayenne and cook, stirring occasionally, until the
   vegetables soften, 10 to 15 minutes.

2. Add the garlic and cook for about a minute more, stirring
   occasionally, until fragrant.

3. Add the wine and Pernod and bring to a boil, scraping up
   any browned bits stuck to the bottom of the pot. Cook for
   about 2 minutes, until the liquid is reduced by half.

Continued

4. Add the seafood stock, tomatoes, orange zest, 1 tablespoon salt, and 1 teaspoon black pepper. Bring to a boil, reduce the heat, and simmer uncovered for 30 minutes, stirring occasionally.

5. Add the mussels, if using, and cook for 2 minutes, then add the fish and continue to simmer until just cooked through, 3 to 4 minutes more. Stir once, very gently, being careful not to break up the fish too much, then ladle into individual serving bowls.

6. To serve: Top each bowl with a sprinkle of parsley, a few fronds of fennel, and a slice of baguette slathered generously with rouille.

Rouille

Makes about 1½ cups

1 garlic clove, minced

¼ teaspoon saffron threads, steeped in ¼ cup boiling water for 5 minutes

1 cup torn white bread, crusts removed

1 tablespoon fresh lemon juice

½ teaspoon cayenne pepper

¾ cup good-quality mayonnaise

¾ cup extra virgin olive oil

Kosher salt

In a food processor or high-speed blender, combine the garlic with the saffron, bread, lemon juice, and cayenne and pulse until blended. Add the mayonnaise and process until smooth. With the machine running, add the oil in a thin stream and blend until emulsified. Transfer the rouille to a bowl and season with salt.

VEGETARIAN BLACK BEAN CHILI 🫘 🌶️

This black bean chili is not only warm, comforting, and spicy, it has additional depth of flavor thanks to coffee and red wine, textural interest from a healthy handful of toasted walnuts, and a smooth, underlying richness from cocoa powder. It's satisfying, packed with protein and fiber, and comes together in a snap.

I love this chili with lots of garnishes such as cilantro, chopped radishes, crumbled cotija cheese, fresh lime, and warm corn tortillas. The chili itself is actually vegan, and you can keep it that way by ignoring some of my suggestions for toppings and sticking to exclusively plant-based choices. Either way, vegans, vegetarians, and carnivores alike will find that this ultra-hearty chili delivers some serious flavor.

Serves 6 to 8

2 tablespoons extra virgin olive oil or coconut oil

1 large yellow onion, diced

2 cloves garlic, minced

2 red or yellow bell peppers, diced

2 teaspoons ground cumin

½ teaspoon cayenne pepper, plus more to taste

1 teaspoon ground paprika

1 teaspoon dried oregano

½ cup dry red wine

½ cup brewed coffee

1½ cups very finely chopped toasted walnuts

5 cups cooked black beans (may use canned beans)

One 28-ounce can whole plum tomatoes

1 cup water

2 teaspoons kosher salt, plus more to taste

2 tablespoons unsweetened natural cocoa powder

Freshly ground black pepper

FOR SERVING

1 bunch fresh cilantro, coarsely chopped

½ cup plain yogurt or sour cream

Shredded Cheddar and/or crumbled cotija cheese

1 lime, quartered

4 corn tortillas, toasted

1. Heat the olive oil in a large heavy-bottomed saucepan or Dutch oven over medium heat. Add the onion, garlic, and bell peppers and cook, stirring occasionally, until the vegetables soften, about 10 minutes.

2. Add the cumin, cayenne, paprika, and oregano and cook for about 1 minute more, stirring occasionally, until fragrant.

3. Add the wine and coffee and bring to a boil, scraping up any browned bits stuck to the bottom of the pot. Cook for about 2 minutes, until the liquid is slightly reduced.

4. Add the walnuts, beans, tomatoes, water, and salt. Bring to a boil, then reduce to a simmer and cook for 30 minutes more.

5. Stir in the cocoa powder, taste, and season with salt and freshly ground pepper, as desired.

6. Serve with assorted toppings, if desired.

CHOCOLATE PASTA WITH BROWN BUTTER, PEARS, AND HAZELNUTS

By this point on our cocoa-dusted journey together, I'm sure we can agree that chocolate really doesn't have to mean dessert. This beautiful pasta dish is one of my favorite ways to demonstrate just how savory cocoa can get. Loosely inspired by recipes common in the Umbria and Tuscany regions of Italy, cocoa powder is added to simple pasta dough, giving it a hint of the rich, intense, earthy, and complex flavor of chocolate—but without the sweetness.

I sometimes like to pair it with other earthy ingredients such as mushrooms, blue cheese, and rosemary, which complement the depth of the chocolate. But this recipe pairing is my favorite. The subtle, toasted flavor and aroma of the pasta is a lovely accompaniment to the nuttiness of the brown butter and hazelnut garnish. The sweet pears play off the cocoa's bitter flavor, creating a balance that just works.

While the idea of making fresh pasta by hand may seem intimidating, *please* don't let that get in your way! I've given you instructions for doing it by hand, which requires absolutely no special ingredients, but I almost always make mine in the food processor. It takes all of about 2 minutes. As for rolling out the noodles, as you'll see below, you can do this with a pasta machine, a sharp knife, or even a pizza roller. It's much less of an undertaking than you'd expect, I promise.

Serves 4

1¾ cups all-purpose flour

¼ cup unsweetened cocoa powder, plus more for dusting

½ teaspoon kosher salt

3 large eggs

1 tablespoon extra virgin olive oil

FOR THE SAUCE

½ cup plus 2 tablespoons unsalted butter

1 medium pear, cored and cut into ½-inch dice

12 large fresh sage leaves, cut into thin ribbons

Kosher salt

FOR SERVING

⅓ cup toasted, chopped hazelnuts

1½ tablespoons cocoa nibs

Freshly grated Parmigiano-Reggiano

To make the pasta

1. Whisk together the flour, cocoa, and salt. On a clean countertop or very large cutting board, turn out the flour mixture and make a well in the middle with your hands.

2. Whisk the eggs and olive oil together in a small bowl until combined, then pour the mixture into the well. Using a fork, whisk the eggs, slowly incorporating the flour bit by bit into the eggs by moving your fork along the edges of the well.

3. When most of the flour is incorporated, begin using your hands to bring the dough together, gently kneading it until it is smooth and elastic, 7 to 10 minutes.

Continued

4. Alternatively, add all the ingredients to a food processor and process until it forms a ball, keeping extra flour and water nearby to adjust the consistency as needed.

5. Wrap the dough in plastic wrap and let it rest at room temperature for about 30 minutes.

6. After resting, knead the dough a few more times, then roll it out until it is very thin and cut it into thin strips. You can either roll it out thinly with a rolling pin and cut it into strips with a sharp knife or pizza cutter, or use a pasta machine.

7. Transfer the cut pasta to a baking sheet and dust it lightly with cocoa powder to keep it from sticking.

8. To cook the pasta, bring a large pot of heavily salted water to a boil. Add the pasta and stir to keep it from clumping. Cook for 2 to 3 minutes, or for about 30 seconds after it comes to the surface. Drain the pasta, reserving ½ cup of the pasta cooking water, and set aside.

To make the sauce

1. Melt the butter in a large sauté pan over medium heat. Continue cooking the butter until the milk solids have turned brown and the butter is caramel colored and smells nutty.

2. Add the pear and sage and toss to combine. Season with salt to taste. Add the pasta to the pan and toss to combine, adding a bit of reserved pasta water if it seems dry.

To serve

Divide the pasta among serving plates. Sprinkle with the hazelnuts, cocoa nibs, and cheese. Serve immediately.

Dressings, Drizzles, Spreads, and Sauces

BOURBON PEACH BBQ SAUCE

I am well aware that barbecue sauce is one of those things that brings about strong feelings. There's the whole Kansas City BBQ vs. Memphis BBQ thing. There's the dry rub vs. mop argument. From sauce-free-Texas to vinegar-based-Carolina, there are a lot of impassioned opinions about where, when, if, and how 'cued meat should or shouldn't be sauced. But I've got to come clean and tell you that I truly don't have a dog in that fight. I mean, is it really so terrible to like *all* the different versions of BBQ?

No matter your BBQ allegiance, I'm pretty sure you're going to like this sweet-and-spicy sauce. It's not *too* sweet, a bit vinegary, bright, and balanced. The peaches lend a mellow, summer-y sweetness, the bourbon adds a kick, and the cayenne, of course, adds BBQ's mandatory spiciness. Making this recipe in the summer when peaches are at their prime (or even a touch past their prime) is best, but if you can't get fresh peaches, you've got a few good options: 1) You can use thawed frozen peaches; 2) You can sub in a different stone fruit such as cherries, plums, or even mango; or 3) If you're making the sauce in the fall, use apples instead of peaches and add ½ teaspoon of cinnamon for a warm, autumnal vibe.

Makes about 3 cups

1 tablespoon olive oil

½ cup diced yellow onion

1 teaspoon minced garlic

1½ cups roughly chopped, peeled fresh peaches

¾ cup ketchup

½ cup bourbon

⅓ cup dark brown sugar

⅓ cup apple cider vinegar

¼ cup molasses

2 tablespoons Dijon mustard

2 tablespoons Worcestershire sauce

½ teaspoon cayenne pepper, plus more to taste

Kosher salt

1. Heat the olive oil in a medium saucepan over medium heat. Add the onion and cook until it has softened, about 5 minutes. Add garlic and cook until fragrant, about 30 seconds.

2. Add the peaches, ketchup, bourbon, brown sugar, vinegar, molasses, mustard, Worcestershire, and cayenne and stir to combine. Bring the mixture to a boil, reduce the heat, and simmer until thickened to your liking, 15 to 20 minutes. Taste and adjust salt and cayenne, as desired.

3. Carefully transfer the sauce to a blender or use an immersion blender to blend until smooth. Add more water, a tablespoon or two at a time, if you prefer a thinner sauce.

4. Let cool to room temperature, transfer to a jar, squeeze bottle, or whatever container you prefer, and store in the refrigerator for up to a month or in the freezer for up to 3 months.

COCOA CHIPOTLE SALSA 🍫

What's better than chips and salsa? Not much! As an accompaniment to drinks, an afternoon snack, appetizer, or as part of a party spread, chips and salsa are a go-to for a reason; they're just so munchable. And, sure, there are plenty of really good jarred salsas out there that make for a convenient snack, but from where I sit, nothing beats homemade salsa. Simple pico de gallo, with fresh tomatoes, jalapeño, onion, and plenty of cilantro and lime, is probably what I make most often when fresh tomatoes are in season. But sometimes I crave good, homemade salsa when tomatoes *aren't* in season. And, thankfully, I've got this gem in my back pocket.

It's a bit more complex, more layered, and more nuanced than my beloved pico de gallo. Combining earthy cocoa, spicy, smoky chipotle, and canned tomatoes (yep, that's right), this salsa is rich yet surprisingly refreshing. And what's best is that you can chuck all the ingredients in the food processor and have ready-to-go salsa in mere minutes. It's a bit more effort than twisting the lid off a jar . . . but not by much.

Makes 4 cups

1 (28-ounce) can whole peeled tomatoes

1 cup loosely packed fresh cilantro

½ small red onion, roughly chopped

2 tablespoons freshly squeezed lime juice, plus more as needed (about 1 lime)

1 cloves garlic, roughly chopped

¼ teaspoon kosher salt, plus more to taste

¼ cup chipotle peppers in adobo sauce

1 tablespoon unsweetened natural cocoa powder

1. Combine all ingredients in a food processor or blender. Pulse in 2-second pulses, scraping down the sides as needed until it is as chunky or smooth as you like it.

2. Taste and adjust salt and/or lime, as desired. Transfer to a serving bowl and refrigerate for at least 30 minutes or up to 1 week.

SPICY BEER CHEESE

There's a restaurant near where I live that serves one of the biggest pretzels I've ever seen—bigger than a dinner plate. I can't tell you what else is on their appetizer menu because I've literally never ordered anything else. And while it's a really, really good pretzel, its deliciousness is nearly eclipsed by two things: 1) the spectacle of it being presented at the table dangling from a giant metal hook, and 2) the fantastic beer cheese that accompanies it. Creamy, tangy, rich, and spicy, I could lick that bowl. All of which is to say that this local gastro pub has reminded me how beer cheese is something I need to have in my life on a regular basis. You do, too. Trust me. At the end of the day, it's a pretty basic cheese sauce that gets most of its amazing flavor from beer, mustard, cayenne, and sharp Cheddar. All it takes is a few ingredients and about 20 minutes or so to make a fast—and tasty—appetizer or snack. Serve it warm with sliced apples and, obviously, pretzels.

Serves 8

2 tablespoons butter

¼ cup all-purpose flour

½ cup whole milk

One 12-ounce bottle beer, such as pale ale or brown ale

4 ounces cream cheese, room temperature

1 tablespoon Dijon mustard

1 teaspoon Worcestershire sauce

½ teaspoon cayenne pepper, plus more to taste

1 pound sharp Cheddar cheese, grated

Kosher salt

1. Melt the butter in a large saucepan over medium heat. Sprinkle the flour on top and cook, stirring constantly for about 1 minute until it resembles wet sand.

2. Whisk in the milk and the beer, then simmer for 5 to 7 minutes, stirring occasionally, until the mixture has thickened.

3. Stir in the cream cheese, mustard, Worcestershire sauce, and cayenne until the cream cheese is melted and the mixture is smooth.

4. Reduce heat to low. Add the Cheddar, stirring until it is completely melted. Season with salt to taste.

5. Serve immediately.

HOMEMADE TABASCO-STYLE HOT SAUCE 🌶

Whether you're staring down a bumper crop of homegrown cayenne peppers, looking for a homemade edible gift, or you've just got a hankering for a bit of DIY, making hot sauce is a fun and doable kitchen project. You'll use the finished product in all kinds of recipes from Buffalo wings to egg dishes, cocktails to tacos. The technique is almost unbelievably simple: It's just a matter of boiling hot peppers with vinegar, garlic, and salt, then blending it all until smooth. One word of warning, though: Please take care not to inhale the fumes or let them get near your eyes. Ever heard of pepper spray? Um, yeah. Be careful! Open a window or put on a snorkel mask or something, OK?

Makes about 2 cups

20 fresh cayenne peppers, stemmed and halved

1½ cups distilled white vinegar or apple cider vinegar

½ teaspoon kosher salt

3 tablespoons minced fresh garlic

1. Put all the ingredients in a medium saucepan. Bring to a boil. Reduce to a simmer and cook, stirring occasionally, until the garlic and chiles have softened, about 15 minutes.

2. Remove the pot from the heat and allow the pepper mixture to cool slightly. Transfer to a blender and puree.

3. Pour the sauce through a fine sieve into a small bowl; discard the solids. Allow the hot sauce to cool completely, then divide it among small bottles or pour into an airtight container. Store in the refrigerator for up to 3 months.

CREOLE SAUCE 🌶

Once upon a time, making dinner was a relaxing affair with nice music playing in the background, usually a glass of wine in hand, and often civilized conversation about the day's happenings with my husband. I'd planned ahead. Or not. Maybe on my way home, I'd pick up a nice piece of fish on a whim. Just because. Doesn't that sound lovely? Now, two kids later (with sports schedules, afterschool activities, playdates, homework, and a house that constantly looks like the Crayola factory exploded in our midst), making dinner requires considerable advance planning, dexterity, efficiency, intense focus, and the ability to make a meal while being subjected to blaring Kidz Bop music. As such, keeping a few simple, flavorful sauces on hand is key for getting food on the table under the gun.

To that end, I stash a variety of sauces in my freezer, such as homemade marinara, pesto, and this Creole sauce, and use them to add quick flavor to all kinds of meals: grilled chicken, fish, meatballs, pasta, even eggs.

Like most Creole recipes, this one starts with the holy trinity of vegetables—onion, bell peppers, and celery—then it comes to life with tomatoes, herbs, and cayenne and gets an infusion of richness from the addition of butter. The end result is a versatile, fresh-tasting, spicy, and complex sauce that you'll be grateful to have in your back pocket (or your freezer) the next time you realize you've got to be at lacrosse practice in 30 and dinner's somehow got to happen between now and then.

Makes about 4 cups

2 tablespoons olive oil

1 medium onion, diced

2 celery stalks, diced

1 medium bell pepper, diced

3 cloves garlic, minced

One 14-ounce can
  diced tomatoes

2 cups chicken stock,
  vegetable stock, or water

1 tablespoon Louisiana-style
  hot sauce, homemade (see
  page 116) or store-bought

2 tablespoons
  Worcestershire sauce

1 teaspoon kosher salt

¼ teaspoon freshly
  ground black pepper

¼ teaspoon cayenne pepper

½ teaspoon dried
  thyme leaves

4 tablespoons butter

½ cup chopped green onions

1. Heat the oil in a large saucepan over medium-high heat.
   Add the onion, celery, and bell pepper and cook, stirring
   occasionally, until vegetables are soft, 3 to 5 minutes. Stir
   in garlic and cook until fragrant, about 30 seconds.

2. Add the tomatoes with their juice, stock, hot sauce,
   Worcestershire sauce, salt, black pepper, cayenne, and
   thyme. Bring the mixture to a boil, then reduce heat to low
   and simmer until it thickens, about 20 minutes.

3. Stir in the butter, green onions, and more hot sauce, if
   desired.

4. Store in a sealed container in the refrigerator for up to
   1 week or in the freezer for up to 3 months.

COCOA-LACED DUKKAH 🍫

Dukkah is an Egyptian mixture of spices, nuts, and seeds; it's used as a versatile seasoning, a condiment, even a snack all on its own. It's traditionally made by pounding cumin, coriander, sesame seeds, salt, dried herbs, and nuts or peanuts in a mortar and pestle (or food processor these days) until it becomes sort of a chunky powder that adds a pop of flavor and texture to all sorts of dishes.

I like it sprinkled over hummus, mixed into yogurt, as a topping for soups and salads, and a crust for seared meat. You can purchase ready-made dukkah, but it's so easy to make at home, plus you can customize it any way you like. You can vary the nuts, switch up the spices, and play around with add-ins, as I've done below. The cocoa nibs here add amazing depth, texture, and a beautiful roasted flavor that complements myriad dishes. Try dipping good bread in a dish of extra virgin olive oil and then into a dish of this mixture for my all-time favorite way to dukkah. (Yep, I just made it a verb.)

Makes about ¾ cup spice mix

¼ cup chopped toasted nuts (I recommend almonds, pistachios, walnuts, or a combination)

1 tablespoon coriander seeds

1 tablespoon cumin seeds

3 tablespoons sesame seeds

¼ teaspoon black peppercorns

⅓ cup (1½ ounces) roasted cocoa nibs

1 teaspoon kosher salt

1. Using a small dry skillet over low heat, toast the nuts for 3 to 5 minutes until fragrant. Next, add the coriander and cumin and toast for a few minutes more. Add the sesame seeds and peppercorns to the skillet and toast those for one minute more, keeping a close eye on it so that nothing burns. Remove the skillet from the heat and mix in the cocoa nibs and salt. Allow the mixture to cool completely.

2. Transfer the dukkah mixture to a mortar and pestle or a food processor and crush until it becomes crumbly (but don't allow it to become a paste).

3. Stored in an airtight container away from heat and direct sunlight, the dukkah can be kept for up to 2 weeks.

ALL-PURPOSE CAYENNE MARINADE 🌶

This easy, all-purpose marinade is often the answer when grilling around here. The whole operation takes mere minutes and really is a dump-and-shake-in-a-jar kind of brainless undertaking. I often double or triple the recipe and store a spare batch in the fridge for last-minute dinner emergencies. (It keeps for ages.) But because it's made entirely from ingredients I typically have on hand, it can also be made on the fly, which is never a bad thing.

The best part, of course, is that it's delicious, elevating all manner of otherwise-ho-hum proteins to crowd-pleasing showstoppers. Brown sugar adds a touch of sweetness and little bits of crunchy caramelization, while the cayenne brings not only a hit of spice, but a shiny brightness that sings against the earthiness of the soy sauce, cumin, and smoked paprika. If you get your act together ahead of time, marinate whatever you plan to grill for at least 6 hours (or overnight), although I've been known to marinate it for as little as 30 minutes and it still turns out a tasty meal. Try this on meat, poultry, seafood or—my favorite—sweet potatoes, either on the grill or in the oven.

Makes about ¾ cup, enough for about
2 pounds of protein or vegetables

¼ cup olive oil

¼ cup loosely packed
brown sugar

2 tablespoons soy sauce

2 tablespoons
Worcestershire sauce

2 tablespoons apple
cider vinegar

2 teaspoons chili powder

2 teaspoons ground cumin

1 teaspoon smoked paprika

¼ to ½ teaspoon cayenne
pepper, or to taste

2 cloves garlic, minced

2 teaspoons kosher salt

1. Combine all ingredients in a jar or bowl. Whisk or shake
to combine.

2. Use it as a marinade for meat or vegetables. Grill, broil,
or bake as desired.

COCOA HAZELNUT SPREAD

Let me be 100 percent clear from the get-go: This is a home-made version of Nutella spread and it is freaking delicious. It's made with very few ingredients, all of which are, more or less, everyday foods (no weird palm oil, for example) and can be used in nearly infinite ways to make life sweeter, chocolaty-er, and all around much better. Oh, and healthier! I don't even think that's so much of a stretch because we're mostly talking about protein-rich and healthy fat-packed nuts and antioxidant-rich cocoa powder. Yes, I call for some powdered sugar (but not a ton); I like the consistency it gives. You could certainly swap in another sweetener such as coconut sugar, agave, or honey if you prefer. I do recommend seeking out hazelnut oil, which is readily available in most well-stocked supermarkets these days, as it amps up the nutty deliciousness of this spread, but any neutral oil would work OK as a substitution. If you're any-thing like me, you'll find yourself eating this stuff straight out of the jar, although I do recommend saving some for adding to smoothie bowls, smearing on toast, stirring into hot cocoa, fill-ing sandwich cookies, swirling into brownies . . . I could go all day, folks. The point being that this stuff is crazy-good and you should go make some. Like, right now. Go on. Go!

Makes about 1½ cups

1 cup toasted, blanched hazelnuts

¼ cup unsweetened natural cocoa powder

½ cup confectioners' sugar

¾ teaspoon vanilla extract

¼ teaspoon kosher salt

4 tablespoons hazelnut or neutral oil

1. Place the hazelnuts in your food processor and process until they turn into a smooth butter, about 3 minutes. Add the remaining ingredients and blend until smooth and creamy.

2. Store in the refrigerator for up to 2 weeks.

SPICY PEANUT SAUCE 🌶

I have always loved the convenience of recipes made from pantry staples, but it wasn't until the COVID-19 lockdown—when getting groceries was so difficult—that I really came to appreciate what a lifesaver a pantry meal can be. After one-too-many beans and rice and pasta with red sauce dinners, I needed to switch things up. This peanut sauce—creamy, rich, savory, a bit sweet, and plenty spicy, thanks to a healthy hit of cayenne—became my saving grace. Not only is it made almost entirely from pantry staples, it's also entirely no-cook, requiring nothing more than a little chopping and shaking or whisking. My favorite ways to serve it are alongside satay-style chicken skewers, drizzled over cold noodles, or thinned out with a couple of tablespoons of water and tossed with shredded chicken, carrots, Napa cabbage, and scallions for a quick and easy salad. But that's just scratching the surface of what this magical sauce can do. Make it once and I think you'll see what I mean . . .

Makes about 1 cup

2 tablespoons tamari
  or soy sauce

2 teaspoons rice vinegar

2 teaspoons honey

1 teaspoon grated
  fresh ginger

1 clove garlic, finely minced
  or grated on a microplane

½ to 1 teaspoon cayenne
  pepper, or to taste

¼ cup creamy peanut butter

3 tablespoons olive oil

2 teaspoons toasted
  sesame oil

Warm water, as needed

1. Place the soy sauce, vinegar, honey, ginger, garlic, and cayenne in a jar or bowl and whisk or shake to combine.

2. Add the peanut butter and whisk or shake again to combine. Add the olive oil and sesame oil and whisk or shake vigorously until the sauce comes together.

3. If the sauce is too thick, add warm water a teaspoon at a time, shaking or whisking between additions, until you achieve the desired consistency.

COCOA VINAIGRETTE

We've all seen the meme: "Chocolate comes from a bean and beans are vegetables; therefore chocolate is salad." Sure, laugh it up, but in this case, chocolate really *is* salad! (Part of it, anyway.) Subtle, a little unexpected, slightly spicy, and completely addictive, this easy vinaigrette is your naked salad greens' new best friend. How about peppery greens, such as arugula or a sweet, salty, colorful tangle of greens, fruit, toasted nuts, and a bit of cheese (think strawberries, fresh mozzarella, mint, and almonds) drizzled with this insane chocolate dressing? Chocolate for dinner! Yay!!

Makes about 1½ cups

½ cup balsamic vinegar

¾ cup extra virgin olive oil

1 tablespoon unsweetened natural cocoa powder

2 tablespoons maple syrup

1 teaspoon minced garlic

¼ teaspoon cayenne pepper

1 teaspoon sea salt

½ teaspoon freshly ground black pepper

1. Combine vinegar, olive oil, cocoa, maple syrup, garlic, cayenne, salt, and pepper in a blender. Process until smooth.

2. Store in the refrigerator in an airtight container for up to 2 weeks.

Baked and Sweet Things

CHOCOLATE BREAD

Not to be confused with chocolate quick bread, which resembles a giant muffin baked in a loaf pan, this chocolate bread is more or less "regular" bread dough that has been flavored with cocoa powder and adorned with chunks of chocolate. It's decidedly *not* dessert, despite being enriched with butter and sugar. It has a subtle chocolate flavor without being too sweet, so it's just right with a cup of coffee, toasted, and spread with butter for breakfast. Not that it *couldn't* become dessert. Serving a warmed slice with a scoop of ice cream, some fresh berries, and a drizzle of chocolate sauce would definitely not be a terrible idea. Beyond that, I probably don't need to wax poetic about all you can spread on or do with chocolate bread, but I'd be remiss if I didn't mention bread pudding, French toast, and the mind-blowingly delicious chocolate, raspberry, and brie grilled cheese sandwich that you now probably want to make right this second. Uh huh! This recipe works particularly well with bread flour, which gives it a really nice rise, but if you don't have it, all-purpose flour absolutely works.

Makes one 9-inch loaf

Continued

2 cups all-purpose
or bread flour

¼ cup unsweetened Dutch-
processed cocoa powder

⅓ cup granulated sugar

¾ cup water, room
temperature

2½ teaspoons instant yeast

4 tablespoons unsalted
butter, melted and
cooled slightly

3 ounces good-quality
dark chocolate,
melted and cooled

1 large egg

¾ teaspoon kosher salt
or coarse sea salt

½ teaspoon vanilla extract

¾ cup chocolate chips
or chunks

Optional add-ins: ½ cup
toasted, chopped nuts;
½ cup dried fruit
(cherries, figs, and
apricots are really lovely);
1 teaspoon grated orange
zest; ½ cup cocoa nibs

1. Butter a 9-inch loaf pan.

2. In the bowl of a heavy-duty stand mixer or a large mixing
   bowl, combine 1 cup flour, cocoa powder, sugar, water,
   yeast, melted butter, melted chocolate, egg, and vanilla.
   Stir using a wooden spoon or the paddle attachment of
   your mixer. Add the remaining flour, stirring until completely incorporated.

3. Switch to the mixer's dough hook and knead for 5 to 7 minutes, until you achieve a smooth dough. If making by hand,
   continue to mix with a wooden spoon. The dough will be
   too sticky for you to knead by hand. No problem!

4. Add the chocolate chips and continue mixing until completely combined, 2 to 3 minutes.

5. Cover the bowl with plastic wrap or a kitchen towel and allow it to rise in a warm place for 2 to 3 hours, until doubled in size.

6. With a spatula or buttered hands, gently deflate the dough, fold it over onto itself a few times, then transfer to the buttered pan. Loosely cover and allow it to rise for one hour.

7. Position a rack in the center of the oven. Preheat to 350°F.

8. Bake the bread for 35 to 40 minutes, until it has a slightly hollow sound when you tap it with your finger.

9. Cool completely on a wire rack. Store at room temperature, wrapped tightly in plastic, up to 3 days or freeze up to 1 month.

SIMPLEST COCOA BROWNIES

Here's something the world probably doesn't need: another brownie recipe. And yet, here you go, because—*seriously*—what would a book about cocoa be without a brownie recipe?! A joke, that's what! And if there's one thing I'm very serious about, it's brownies. They're my absolute favorite dessert and—philosophical disputes aside—I like them in all their forms. Fudgy, chewy, cakey . . . basically, I'll take 'em any way I can get 'em. (Although, in the middle vs. edge debate, I am all about the squidgy middles.) I've made some pretty elaborate brownies in my day with chunks and drizzles, frostings, and even left-over Halloween candy—all irresistible. But sometimes what you need is a simple, pantry-based, so-easy-a-monkey-could-make-it brownie recipe, and that, friends, is what we have here.

The best part is that you don't need a mixer and they're made in only one bowl! Plus, they're deeply chocolatey (interestingly, cocoa powder has more pure chocolate flavor than actual chocolate because there's no milk or sugar getting in the way) and super rich. Also, you're not going to end up with a dinky 8-by-8-inch pan. *Please!* This recipe calls for a 9-by-13-inch because the more brownies, the better. You can use natural or Dutch-processed cocoa in this recipe, as there's no leavening agent to complicate matters, but I prefer the flavor of natural cocoa here. Either way, use the best-quality cocoa powder you have, because that's the predominant flavor and you want these suckers to knock your socks off.

Continued

Makes about 24 brownies

1 cup (2 sticks)
  unsalted butter

1 cup unsweetened
  cocoa powder

1 cup granulated sugar

1 cup dark brown sugar

4 large eggs

2 teaspoons vanilla extract

½ cup all-purpose flour

⅛ teaspoon kosher salt

1. Line a 9-by-13-by-2-inch pan with parchment or greased foil. Preheat the oven to 325°F.

2. Melt the butter and cocoa powder in a large microwave-safe bowl or in a large saucepan on the stovetop. Add the granulated and brown sugars, beating well with a wooden spoon. Add the eggs one at a time, and beat until the mixture is smooth and shiny. Stir in the vanilla extract.

3. Mix in the flour and salt, stirring until smooth, then spread the batter into the prepared pan.

4. Bake 30 to 40 minutes, until the brownies are set and a toothpick inserted in the center comes out with moist crumbs (not wet batter). Cool completely on a rack before cutting. Oh, who are we kidding? Just try not to burn your fingers while getting hot brownies out of the pan and into your mouth.

NOT-TOO-SWEET CHOCOLATE BISCOTTI 🍫

These crisp, crunchy, twice-baked Italian cookies are just the thing to have around when you need more than *just* a cup of coffee. They're sweet enough, but not so sweet that you couldn't call them breakfast if you really wanted to justify dunking them into your morning latte. They're also perfect for dipping into sherry, brandy, and—my favorite—red wine, which plays beautifully with chocolate. I've given you directions for making these in a food processor, which is my preferred method, as it's lightning-fast and super easy, although they're easy enough to make by hand or in a stand mixer.

I've stuck with pure chocolate-on-chocolate for flavoring these biscotti, but feel free to customize them if you like. You can mix in nuts, such as hazelnuts, pistachios, or almonds, in place of some or all of the chocolate. And if dried fruit is your thing, dried cherries would be fantastic. But if you really want to take things over the top, you can half-dip the biscotti in melted chocolate, then let them cool until the chocolate hardens.

Makes about 50 cookies

2 cups flour

¾ cup unsweetened cocoa powder

1 teaspoon baking soda

½ teaspoon kosher salt

¾ cup granulated sugar

½ cup packed brown sugar

4 tablespoons butter, softened

2 teaspoons vanilla extract

4 large eggs, at room temperature

1 cup chocolate chips or chunks

Continued

1. Preheat the oven to 350°F. Line a baking sheet with parchment paper.

2. In a small bowl, whisk together the flour, cocoa, baking soda, and salt; set aside.

3. **To make by hand**: In a large mixing bowl, cream the sugars and butter, until light and fluffy. Add the vanilla extract and stir until thoroughly incorporated. Add 3 of the eggs one at a time, beating after each addition, until smooth. Add the flour mixture and mix until the dough is uniform and sticky. Stir in the chocolate chips.

4. **To make in a food processor**: Combine the sugars and butter in the work bowl of the food processor. Process 30 seconds, until smooth. Add the vanilla extract and pulse to combine. Add 3 of the eggs one at a time, processing until smooth after each addition. Add the flour mixture and let the machine run until a sticky dough comes together. Add chocolate chips and pulse 5 to 6 times, until the chips are evenly incorporated.

5. On a lightly floured surface, with floured hands, roll the dough into two logs, approximately 12-by-2 inches. Transfer the logs to the baking sheet and flatten slightly.

6. In a small bowl, make an egg wash by beating the 1 remaining egg with 1 tablespoon water. Brush the tops of the logs with the egg wash, then put the baking sheet in the oven. Bake the dough for 20 to 25 minutes, until firm to the touch.

7. Remove the dough from the oven and cool for 30 minutes. Transfer the logs to a cutting board and, using a serrated knife, cut the logs into ½-inch slices. Return the cookies to the baking sheet, laying them cut side down, and return them to the oven for another 20 minutes, until they are crisp.

8. Cool completely before serving or storing in an airtight container for up to 2 weeks.

MEXICAN HOT CHOCOLATE SHORTBREAD

These melt-in-your-mouth, crumbly chocolate cookies, spiced with cinnamon and cayenne, are evocative of Mexican drinking chocolate. Almond extract adds sweet complexity to the flavor, but I know people either love it or hate it, so if almond isn't your thing, you can leave it out. And while I've set the heat level at a fairly moderate place—you'll certainly notice the cayenne, but it won't blow the roof off—if you feel compelled to dial it up a bit, you can increase it to 1 teaspoon. The chocolate chips here add both texture and additional chocolate flavor to the cookies, but you *could* swap them out for cocoa nibs if you really wanted to deepen the bitter flavor and add some crunch. However, no matter how you customize these cookies, they're great for gifting, as they keep for ages. Wrapped well, they'll keep for as long as 3 to 4 weeks.

Makes 24 to 36 cookies

1 cup (2 sticks) unsalted butter, at room temperature

½ teaspoon vanilla extract

½ teaspoon almond extract (optional)

1 cup packed dark brown sugar

½ cup unsweetened Dutch-processed cocoa powder

½ teaspoon ground cinnamon

½ teaspoon kosher salt

¼ teaspoon cayenne pepper

1½ cups all-purpose flour

½ cup semisweet or milk chocolate chips

1. Line two cookie sheets with parchment.

2. In the bowl of a stand mixer fitted with the paddle attachment or in a large mixing bowl using a handheld mixer, cream the butter, vanilla, and almond extract (if using) for about 2 minutes, until the mixture is pale and fluffy. Add the brown sugar, cocoa, cinnamon, salt, and cayenne pepper, and continue to beat for another 2 minutes, until the mixture is smooth. Gradually add the flour, mixing just until combined. Stir in the chocolate chips.

3. Turn the dough out onto a sheet of wax paper or parchment and press into a log about 12 inches long. Roll the log up in the wax paper and refrigerate for at least one hour or until firm.

4. Preheat the oven to 325°F.

5. Remove the dough from the paper and, using a very sharp knife, slice into ¼-inch-thick slices.

6. Bake the cookies on parchment-lined sheet pans, for 15 to 18 minutes, until firm.

7. Cool completely on wire racks, then serve or store in an airtight container for 3 to 4 weeks at room temperature.

SPICY CHOCOLATE CAKE WITH MOCHA BUTTERCREAM

This cake is a riff on a wacky cake recipe I wrote about in my first cookbook, *The Apple Cider Vinegar Companion.* The recipe became popular during World War II when homemakers needed to find a way to bake without breaking into their rations (such as eggs, milk, and butter). Instead, they used oil, vinegar, and water to turn out moist, delicious chocolate cakes that just so happened to be dairy-free and egg-free. It's one of my favorite, quick cake recipes, not only for the ease with which it comes together (seriously, almost as easy as boxed mix), but also for the light, moist, and chocolatey result. So, this is that cake, doctored up a bit.

I've added cinnamon and cayenne for some warmth and kick and have paired it with a really good mocha buttercream. Even coffee skeptics like this frosting, as it isn't really coffee flavored so much as the coffee in it adds to the dark, rich nature of the chocolate. I like to make this cake in a Bundt pan, as described below, but you could divide the batter and bake it in two 8- or 9-inch cake pans for 35 to 45 minutes. You'll want to double the buttercream recipe to fill and frost a layer cake, though.

Serves 10 to 12

FOR THE CAKE

3 cups all-purpose flour, plus more for dusting

⅔ cup unsweetened Dutch-processed cocoa powder

2 cups granulated sugar

2 teaspoons baking soda

2 teaspoons kosher salt

1 teaspoon ground cinnamon

¼ to ½ teaspoon cayenne pepper

2 cups water

1 cup vegetable oil

2 teaspoons pure vanilla extract, or 1 teaspoon almond extract

2 tablespoons apple cider vinegar

FOR THE FROSTING

¾ cup unsalted butter, softened

½ cup unsweetened natural or Dutch-processed cocoa powder

2½ cups confectioners' sugar

¼ cup milk

1 teaspoon vanilla extract

1 tablespoon espresso powder

To Make the Cake

1. Preheat the oven to 350°F.

2. Generously grease and flour a 9-inch Bundt pan.

3. In a large bowl, whisk together flour, cocoa powder, sugar, baking soda, salt, cinnamon, and cayenne pepper. Pour in the water, vegetable oil, vanilla, and vinegar, whisking thoroughly but quickly, until smooth.

4. Pour the batter into the prepared pan and bake for 45 to 50 minutes, until a tester comes out clean and the cake springs back when gently pressed.

Continued

5. Allow to cool in the pan for 10 minutes, then turn out onto a wire rack to cool completely.

To Make the Buttercream

1. In the bowl of a stand mixer fitted with the paddle attachment or in a large mixing bowl, using a handheld mixer, beat the butter on medium speed for 2 minutes until light and fluffy. Add the cocoa and confectioners' sugar and turn your mixer on low, gradually increasing the speed, then beat until the sugar is thoroughly combined with the butter. Add the milk, vanilla extract, and espresso powder, and beat on medium speed for another 3 minutes, or until buttercream becomes light and fluffy.

2. Frost the cooled cake with the buttercream.

DIY HOT COCOA MIX 5 WAYS 🍫 🌶️

I remember when I was finally allowed to make my very own mug of hot cocoa as a kid. I'd carefully add hot water and a packet of Swiss Miss to my favorite mug (the Miss Piggy one), then stir until sweet, steaming delicious cocoa seemed to magically materialize before my eyes. I felt very grown up "cooking" like that. Later on, I learned to make rich, decadent hot chocolate from scratch, with milk and either unsweetened cocoa powder and sugar or melted dark chocolate or both and, well, I kind of didn't look back. That is, until I had kids, who somehow discovered that the world included boxed cocoa mix with crazy unicorn marshmallows and rainbows and—I don't know—glitter? And, of course, they *had* to have it. Then, in a plot twist surprising even to me, I caved and bought it. What can I say? Unicorn marshmallows seemed pretty cool. Also, nostalgia got the best of me.

But here's the thing about store-bought mixes: They're convenient, but that's about it. Rainbow glitter aside, packaged mix yields a cup of cocoa that is kind of flat, watery, and not nearly as chocolatey as I like it. But I've found that same convenience in my own mix, which I keep stashed in our cupboard. It takes all of five minutes to prep, I have total control over what goes into it (and what doesn't) and, most important, it makes a super-rich and delicious cup of nearly instant hot cocoa, which is perfect on a cold day or whenever a case of the grumps hits us. It makes a lovely gift decanted into a pretty jar with a ribbon, and can be easily customized in lots of fun ways, as noted below. I do find

Continued

that giving all the ingredients a buzz in the food processor produces the most pleasing texture, but that step is by no means necessary: Don't let a bit of kitchen machinery get between you and this fabulous homemade cocoa mix. You *can* simply dump all the ingredients into a bowl and whisk until combined.

Makes about 4 cups

1½ cups granulated sugar (may substitute coconut sugar or another sugar of your choosing)

5 ounces bittersweet chocolate, finely chopped

1 cup unsweetened Dutch-processed cocoa powder

1½ cups nonfat dry milk powder

5 teaspoons cornstarch

½ teaspoon kosher salt

Add all the ingredients to the work bowl of a food processor and process 30 to 60 seconds, until ground to a fine powder. Transfer to an airtight container and store at room temperature for up to 3 months.

To Make Hot Cocoa

Combine 2 to 3 tablespoons of cocoa mix with 1 cup hot water or milk in a mug. Whisk or stir until fully incorporated. Serve immediately.

CUSTOMIZE YOUR CUP

Spicy Hot Cocoa Mix: Prepare as above, adding 1 teaspoon ground ancho chile, 1 teaspoon ground cinnamon, and ½ teaspoon cayenne pepper to the mixture.

Pumpkin Spice Hot Cocoa Mix: Prepare as above, adding 1¼ teaspoons cinnamon, ¾ teaspoon fresh grated nutmeg, ½ teaspoon ground ginger, and ¼ teaspoon ground cloves to the mixture.

Espresso Hot Cocoa Mix: Prepare as above, adding ½ cup espresso powder to the mixture.

Peppermint Hot Cocoa Mix: Prepare as above, adding 1 cup finely crushed peppermint candies, such as candy canes or starlight mints.

Earl Grey Hot Cocoa Mix: Prepare as above, adding ½ cup finely ground loose leaf Earl Grey tea to the mixture.

BETTER-THAN-STORE-BOUGHT CHOCOLATE SYRUP

From topping sundaes to flavoring a plain old glass of milk, you can't beat a dark, shiny squeeze of good old-fashioned chocolate syrup. But store-bought chocolate syrup? It's usually cluttered with artificial flavors, junky preservatives, and high-fructose corn syrup, which is actually kind of hard to understand, because at its most basic level, chocolate syrup is nothing more than simple syrup gussied up with some cocoa powder. This homemade chocolate syrup—with cocoa, vanilla, a bit of melted chocolate for body and depth, and a touch of coffee to enhance the chocolate's flavor—is not only easy to make, but way more delicious than anything you can find on a supermarket shelf. It keeps for ages in the fridge, so you might even consider making a double batch. Store it in any kind of lidded container you like; I find a squeeze bottle to be particularly convenient. To make hot cocoa or chocolate milk, whisk two tablespoons of chocolate syrup into 1 cup of hot or cold milk, respectively.

Makes about 2 cups

1½ cups packed dark brown sugar

½ cup water

6 tablespoons unsweetened cocoa powder

1 tablespoon chopped milk chocolate or semisweet chocolate chips

1 tablespoon brewed espresso or strong coffee

¼ teaspoon kosher salt

1 tablespoon vanilla extract

1. In a medium saucepan, combine the brown sugar, water, cocoa, chocolate, coffee, and salt. Whisk over medium heat until the dry ingredients have dissolved, the chocolate has melted, and the mixture is smooth.

2. Continue cooking, whisking occasionally, until the sauce begins to gently boil. Remove from the heat and allow the mixture to cool slightly. Add the vanilla extract and whisk to combine.

3. Store in an airtight container in the refrigerator.

HOMEMADE CHOCOLATE CHEWS (A.K.A. TOOTSIE ROLL-KNOCKOFFS) 🍫

Clearly, it's no secret that I love a good DIY project, but I don't typically *do* homemade candy. You see, I'm not a pastry chef. My professional culinary training did not include much more than the most basic fundamentals of pastry and confections, so truth be told, I'm kind of intimidated by the whole science of sugar, which is something pastry chefs can handle in their sleep. Usually, candy making involves boiling sugar to very precise temperatures and there are many, many opportunities for error. Not that I *can't* make candy—I've made caramels, lollipops, taffy, toffee, and the like—but to varying degrees of success and, *ahem*, burnt cookware . . . . So, this old-school deliciousness is perfect for confectionery blockheads like me because it isn't cooked at all, which makes this not only achievable but painless. In fact, it's a bit like making homemade Play-Doh. Pure fun! The candies are soft, chewy, and delicious, and can even be customized with all sorts of flavorings and extracts. I've suggested a few below, but a teaspoon or so of just about any dried spice or extract you like will almost certainly work here.

Makes 30 to 40 candies

¼ cup unsweetened
   natural cocoa powder

1 cup confectioners' sugar

¼ cup dry milk powder

Pinch of kosher salt

¼ cup light corn syrup

2 tablespoons unsalted
   butter, melted

1 teaspoon pure
   vanilla extract

Optional flavorings:
   ½ teaspoon orange extract,
   1 tablespoon instant
   coffee powder, ½ teaspoon
   peppermint extract

1. In a large bowl, sift together the cocoa powder, confectioners' sugar, dry milk, and salt. Set aside.

2. In a small bowl, whisk together the corn syrup, melted
   butter, vanilla extract, and any other additional flavorings
   you like until completely combined.

3. Add the syrup mixture to the dry ingredients, first stirring with a wooden spoon, then using your hands to knead
   the mixture until smooth. Form the dough into a disc.

4. Using a sharp knife, cut the dough into ½-inch slices. Take
   one slice and roll it into a long, thin rope; cut the rope into
   1-inch pieces. Repeat with remaining dough. Transfer the
   cut candies to a baking sheet and refrigerate for 1 hour
   until firm.

5. Individually wrap the candies in 3-inch square pieces
   of parchment or wax paper. Keep refrigerated for up to
   2 months.

RICH CHOCOLATE TOFU PUDDING

I am forever looking for ways to get more plant protein into my carb-loving kiddos. To that end, I love using multitasking, protein-rich ingredients. Naturally, when I first heard about pudding made from tofu, I was intrigued. Tofu is a fabulous source of plant-based protein and contains all nine essential amino acids. It is also a great source of iron, calcium, manganese, phosphorous, magnesium, copper, zinc, and vitamin B. Talk about a superfood! It's also amazingly versatile, thanks to its neutral flavor, so it works in lots of different kinds of recipes. Tofu exists in several varieties and textures, many of which I cook with regularly. Except for one: silken tofu.

Silken tofu is made similarly to "regular" tofu, but because the soy milk is coagulated but not curdled, the resulting texture is surprisingly smooth. Even better, because making tofu pudding involves putting the whole shebang in the blender, the texture of this pudding is, well, *silky*, smooth, and perfectly creamy. I may be late to the tofu pudding party, but this decadent, deeply chocolaty recipe more than makes up for it.

Serves 4 to 6

1 pound silken tofu

⅔ cup brown sugar

⅓ cup unsweetened cocoa powder

1 cup semisweet chocolate chips, melted

2 teaspoons vanilla extract

Pinch of kosher salt

OPTIONAL GARNISHES

Fresh berries

Sliced almonds

Bananas

Shaved dark chocolate

Cacao nibs

1. Put all ingredients in a food processor or blender. Process until completely smooth.

2. Spoon the pudding into 4 to 6 serving bowls, cover, and chill for at least 30 minutes. Serve, garnished as desired.

SPICY NUT BRITTLE 🌶️

Here's another exception to my no-candy-making rule, as this nut brittle requires no thermometer and is made entirely in the microwave! It really couldn't be easier and turns out a delicious, perfectly spiced, crunchy, and not-too-sticky nut brittle. Peanuts are certainly most classic here, but feel free to use any type or combination of nuts or seeds you like. As always, feel free to adjust the spice level to your liking—just bear in mind that this is the kind of heat that sort of sneaks up on you. At first, you'll taste the sweetness of the candy, then the toasty nut flavor, but the heat will hit you at the end. And as for cleanup, this is sticky stuff! Your bowl will be caked with hardened nut brittle, but don't panic. A good soak in hot soapy water will take care of that in no time. I highly recommend using a silicone spatula to spread the hot candy onto the baking sheet—it will be much easier to clean than a wooden spoon.

Makes about 12 servings

2 cups nuts (peanuts can be dry roasted; all others should be raw)

½ teaspoon cayenne pepper

½ teaspoon cinnamon

1 cup granulated sugar

½ cup light corn syrup

1 teaspoon kosher salt

1 tablespoon unsalted butter

1 teaspoon vanilla extract

1 teaspoon baking soda

1. Line a large rimmed baking sheet with a silicone baking mat or greased parchment paper.

2. Combine the nuts, cayenne, and cinnamon in a bowl. Set aside.

3. Combine the sugar, corn syrup, and salt in a large microwave-safe bowl.

4. Cook on HIGH for 4 minutes. Carefully add the nut mixture, stir to combine, and return the bowl to the microwave to cook on HIGH for 3½ minutes more.

5. Stir in butter and vanilla extract. Return the bowl to the microwave and cook on HIGH for an additional 90 seconds.

6. Remove from the microwave and stir in the baking soda (the mixture will foam). Spoon the brittle onto the prepared baking sheet and spread thinly.

7. Cool the brittle for 30 to 45 minutes and then break into pieces.

CINNAMON-CAYENNE ICE CREAM ◢

Think about a slice of pumpkin pie—ooh, or maybe apple crisp. Now imagine one of those already amazing desserts with a scoop of homemade cinnamon-cayenne ice cream on top. It's almost too much deliciousness to comprehend, I know. Almost. With a brown sugar base, this stuff has dreamy caramel undertones and, of course, the warm spice of cinnamon and gentle heat from the cayenne. It's the perfect complement to all sorts of fall and winter holiday desserts such as gingerbread and apple pie, but it also makes for a fantastic summer treat scooped onto fresh peaches, served alongside plum cake, or sandwiched between graham crackers. I recommend making this in an ice cream machine if you have one, as it not only is easier, but you'll end up with a slightly smoother, creamier ice cream at the end. That said, I have included notes below on how to make this without a machine. With a little more elbow grease, you'll still end up with delicious, creamy ice cream.

Makes about 1 quart

2 cups heavy cream

2 cups milk

¼ cup granulated sugar

¾ cup brown sugar

1 tablespoon ground cinnamon

¼ to ½ teaspoon cayenne pepper

Pinch of kosher salt

8 egg yolks

1. Create an ice bath by filling a large bowl halfway with ice water, then nesting a medium bowl on top. Set a fine-mesh sieve over the medium bowl.

2. Combine 1 cup of the heavy cream, the milk, sugars, cinnamon, cayenne, and salt in a medium saucepan and heat over medium until steaming, stirring frequently to prevent scorching. Remove from the heat.

3. In a small bowl, whisk together the egg yolks, then gradually add about one-third of the warm milk. Pour the mixture back into the saucepan and return it to the heat, stirring constantly, until it thickens and coats the back of a spoon, 5 to 8 minutes.

4. Pour the custard through the sieve into the bowl resting over the ice bath. Add the remaining 1 cup of heavy cream and stir the custard until cool, then cover and refrigerate until cold, 4 to 48 hours.

5. Freeze the custard in your ice cream maker according to the manufacturer's instructions.

Note: To churn ice cream without a machine, make and chill the custard as above, then pour into a sturdy, freezer-safe bowl or baking dish. Place it in the freezer for 45 minutes. Then, with a whisk or handheld electric mixer, beat vigorously to break up the ice crystals that have begun to form and return it to the freezer. Repeat this process every 30 minutes for 3 to 4 hours until it's frozen.

SPICY MANGO ICE POPS 🌶

These Mexican-style ice pops, *paletas*, are inspired by the sweet and spicy mango on a stick that street vendors sell all over Mexico. If you aren't familiar, it's pretty much what it sounds like: fresh, juicy mango that has been peeled, placed on a thick wooden skewer (a *palito*), cut into the shape of a flower, then drizzled with lime juice, salt, and ground chili pepper. It's a fun snack to eat and a great way to cool down on a hot day. Even more refreshing—and less work, let's be honest (I'm pretty fun, but I'm not sure I'm cut-mangos-into-flowers fun)—are these sweet, slightly tart, and delightfully spicy ice pops. Using fresh mangoes when they're in season makes for an especially delicious treat, but you can substitute a 24-ounce bag of frozen mango chunks, thawed, if fresh aren't available.

Makes 4 to 8 pops, depending on the size of your molds

4 medium ripe mangoes (about 3½ pounds)

⅓ cup granulated sugar, or more as needed, depending on sweetness of the mangoes

¼ cup freshly squeezed lime juice

¼ teaspoon chili powder

¼ teaspoon cayenne pepper, or more to taste

⅛ teaspoon fine sea salt

1. Peel and cut the mangoes into large chunks.

2. Combine the mango chunks, sugar, lime juice, spices, and salt in a blender and puree until very smooth. Strain through a fine-mesh sieve. Taste and adjust seasoning, as desired.

3. Divide the mixture among the pop molds and freeze until solid, 4 to 6 hours.

CHEATER'S HOMEMADE CHOCOLATE FROM CACAO NIBS

The idea of harvesting, de-podding, roasting, and creating chocolate from the real, actual beginning is right up my alley and something I'd absolutely *love* to do someday. But there are a few hurdles that I haven't been able to overcome to date. For one thing, whole cacao beans aren't exactly easy to come by if you don't live in a part of the world where they're grown. (And I don't.) Sure, there are suppliers online, but last I checked, cacao pods are really expensive! And when you do find them, there's the whole business of scooping the beans out, fermenting them, roasting them, shelling them . . . it's a whole thing. So, to scratch my wannabe-chocolatier itch, every once in a while, when I'm looking for a fun project, I'll make chocolate "from the bean" using cacao nibs.

Because cacao nibs are bits of fermented, dried, sometimes-roasted, and crushed cacao beans, lots of the upfront work has already been taken care of. All that's left to do, really, is mill and grind the beans with sugar and, before you know it, you'll have made chocolate! Pretty fun. The texture of your chocolate depends highly on how finely you're able to grind the cacao nibs and sugar. A coffee grinder will likely give you the smoothest result, but a high-speed blender or food processor will give you a plenty-good, if slightly gritty, piece of chocolate.

Makes about 1 bar's worth

½ cup cocoa nibs, roasted (see note)

¼ cup granulated sugar

1 tablespoon cocoa butter, melted

Tiny pinch of kosher salt

1. Grind the cocoa nibs in a high-speed blender or food processor until very fine. Pour into a bowl and set aside.

2. Process the sugar until it is also finely ground.

3. Combine the sugar and cocoa nibs in the food processor or blender and blend them together. With the machine running, gradually add the melted cocoa butter and continue blending until the mixture is a smooth liquid.

4. Pour the chocolate into molds (muffin tins lined with parchment or cupcake wrappers work well in place of molds). Refrigerate for about 20 minutes, until set.

Note: If your cocoa nibs are not roasted, preheat your oven to 300°F. Place your cocoa nibs on a large baking sheet and roast them for about 10 minutes, until they've begun to darken and smell decidedly like chocolate.

HEALING TREATMENTS

MAGICAL MORNING TONIC 🌶

I'm a coffee lover, but thanks to an increasingly persnickety digestive system, I've found that coffee isn't always what my body wants or needs first thing in the morning. Instead, matcha, made from powdered green tea leaves, is what I often drink to start the day, as much for its health benefits as its uniquely grassy, sweet flavor and the jitter-free energy boost it gives me. Usually, I have it simply whisked into hot water and occasionally I blend it into steamed almond or coconut milk for a latte-style beverage, but lately I've been turning it into a bracing, energizing tonic with lemon juice, fresh ginger, and a blast of cayenne. It's chock-full of powerful antioxidants, vitamins, and immune-boosting nutrients and tastes great both hot and iced. I am not especially fond of sweet drinks in the morning, but if you like your morning cuppa sweetened, you can stir in some raw honey for flavor and extra health benefits.

Makes 1 serving

1 tablespoon freshly squeezed lemon juice

½ teaspoon freshly grated ginger

⅛ teaspoon cayenne pepper, or to taste

1 to 2 teaspoons raw honey, or to taste (optional)

1 teaspoon matcha powder

1 cup hot, but not boiling, water

Combine the lemon juice, ginger, cayenne, and honey (if using) in a mug or glass; stir well. Add the matcha powder, then the water, and whisk thoroughly to combine. Drink and enjoy.

IMMUNE SUPPORTING TONIC ✐

I always thought medicine was supposed to taste bad. As a kid, that was a fact of life. Except, of course, for the heavenly pink stuff you'd get for ear infections and strep throat. Oh, and orange-flavored chewable baby aspirin. That was delicious. But otherwise, you'd pinch your nose and suck it down, like it or not. So I was very confused when I had to fill my daughter's first prescription for antibiotics and the pharmacist handed me a literal menu of flavors I could have added to the medicine. Banana, watermelon, bubblegum . . . chocolate? Wait, was I supposed to make medicine fun? Somehow that concept still doesn't add up for me. Medicine isn't candy and I don't want my kids to mistake one for the other. That said, I, being an adult of sound mind, know the difference between the two and you'd be hard-pressed to get me to take something horrible-tasting, even when I'm sick.

This concentrated combo of immune-boosting ingredients, each with its own healing properties, mercifully, tastes great. Ginger, turmeric, apple cider vinegar, cayenne pepper, and honey all work together to fight germs and soothe inflammation. Ginger is great for respiratory viruses; turmeric is an overall immunity rock star; apple cider vinegar fights bacteria and helps balance your body's pH levels; cayenne pepper thins out mucus, revs up germ-fighting body temperature, and helps ease pain and inflammation; and raw honey is antiviral, antibacterial, and a fantastic sore throat soother. It's no bottle of pink stuff, but it's warming, soothing, and pleasant to sip when you're feeling down and out.

Continued

Makes 1 treatment

1 cup water

¼ teaspoon ground turmeric
or ½ teaspoon freshly
grated turmeric

¼ teaspoon freshly
grated ginger

⅛ teaspoon cayenne pepper

2 teaspoons apple
cider vinegar

1 tablespoon raw honey

1. Combine water, turmeric, ginger, and cayenne pepper in a small saucepan set over medium heat. Bring the mixture to a boil, reduce the heat, and simmer for 10 to 15 minutes.

2. Strain the liquid into a mug, add in the apple cider vinegar and honey, and stir to combine.

3. Sip while warm.

REJUVENATING ELIXIR 🌶

Whenever I'm feeling sluggish, run down, or suffering the ill-effects of having lived too much of "my best life," I'll start the day with a green juice to give the ol' machine a bit of a reset. Of course, taking a big break from processed foods, meat, sugars, and caffeine for a week or so helps, too, but this fresh, green, and powerful little elixir is a great jumpstart. Celery, which is loaded with antioxidants, including quercetin, caffeic acid, and ferulic acid, lowers inflammation and—because it is a natural diuretic—it helps with bloat. Cilantro (a.k.a. fresh coriander) is super rich in folate, antioxidants, vitamin C, and beta-carotene, which protect against oxidative stress and contribute to a glowing complexion. Cayenne pepper, as we well know, contains detoxifying properties, soothes stomach pain, boosts metabolism, and even benefits cardiovascular health. It's also a powerful anti-inflammatory compound, which contributes to improved circulation and lower blood pressure. A proven digestive aid, ginger contains powerful anti-inflammatory compounds that reduce pain and symptoms of inflammation. The apple is there mostly for taste, but you know what they say about an apple a day. . . . This is easiest made in a juicer, but you can also make it in a blender; see notes below for instructions.

Makes 1 serving

3 stalks celery

1 granny smith apple

1 lime, peeled

Small handful of cilantro

One 1-inch piece fresh ginger

⅛ teaspoon cayenne pepper

1. Juice celery, apple, lime, cilantro, and ginger using a juicer.

2. Pour juice into a glass and stir in the cayenne.

3. Drink immediately or refrigerate in an airtight container for up to 24 hours.

Note: To make the elixir in a blender, blend the celery, apple (cored and peeled), lime, cilantro, ginger, and cayenne, preferably in a high-speed blender, until it looks like a smoothie. If necessary, you may add a small amount of water—¼ cup or so—to get things going. Pour the pureed juice into a fine-mesh sieve lined with cheesecloth or into a nut-milk bag to strain out the pulp.

MEMORY AND BRAIN ENHANCING COCOA

For most of us, cognitive performance—stuff like memory and the ability to easily learn new things—will go through at least some degree of normal, gradual decline as we age. Genetics play a big role in this, but so do environmental, social, and lifestyle factors. Sure, there's little we can do to change our genetics, but we have lots of control over our lifestyle and, as it turns out, enriching it with cocoa might, in fact, have a positive impact on our memory and brain function!

You see, cocoa is rich in flavanols, which have been shown to help lower blood pressure, improve blood flow to the brain and heart, prevent blood clots, and fight cell damage. Studies have shown that flavanol could play an important role in slowing, or even preventing, those declines associated with normal aging. Now at the risk of disappointing those who were just about to reach for a bag of M&M's, most of these studies have looked at the effects of ingesting flavanol supplements or extracts rather than half a pound of Hershey's Kisses.

In our everyday, non-lab-based lives, the best way of getting cocoa flavanols is through cocoa powder that is as natural as possible and has not been Dutch-processed, which removes some of the nutrients. Some research suggests that we should aim for a daily intake of about 200 milligrams of cocoa flavanols, which equates to about 2 tablespoons of natural cocoa powder per day. The recipe below easily meets that

Continued

requirement with both cocoa and dark chocolate plus almond milk (which is rich in vitamin E, an antioxidant associated with the prevention or slowing of cognitive decline) and coconut sugar (which is high in blood-sugar balancing inulin fiber and zinc, which supports brain function and memory). I know it's tough, but sometimes you've just got to take your lumps . . . of MARSHMALLOWS!!

Makes 1 serving

2 tablespoons dark chocolate chips or chunks (at least 74% cacao)

3 tablespoons unsweetened natural cocoa powder

1 to 2 tablespoons coconut sugar (may substitute with another sweetener)

¼ teaspoon pure vanilla extract

Small pinch of sea salt

2 cups unsweetened almond milk (may substitute with another milk of your choosing)

OPTIONAL GARNISHES

Unsweetened cocoa powder

Marshmallows

Dark chocolate shavings

1. Whisk the dark chocolate, cocoa powder, sugar, and salt together in a small saucepan. Add the almond milk and bring the mixture to a low simmer over medium-low heat, whisking often until the chocolate is melted, about 2 minutes. Add the vanilla extract and stir to combine.

2. Ladle the hot cocoa into a mug and garnish as desired.

PMS REDUCING SMOOTHIE 🥥

Cramps, bloating, lethargy, acne, mood swings, and headaches—ugh. These are the all-too-common symptoms of premenstrual syndrome. Treating all that with chocolate may seem a bit cliche, but it turns out that there is actually something to that stereotypical monthly craving. What we eat has a huge impact on our hormones, and the right foods (no, not a bag of salty potato chips or a pint of ice cream) can help balance hormones and decrease those annoying PMS symptoms.

This smoothie is packed with all the goods you need to make PMS a bit easier to deal with. Magnesium-rich cocoa helps with moodiness and promotes relaxation. Adaptogenic maca powder is energizing and balancing. Antioxidant-rich matcha reduces systemic inflammation and, thanks to an amino acid called L-theanine, helps muscles and blood vessels relax, which can reduce cramping. All in all, a tasty solution to a nagging problem.

Serves 1

1½ cups almond milk or other plant-based milk

1 tablespoon cocoa powder

½ teaspoon matcha powder

1 teaspoon maca powder

Maple syrup, to taste

¾ cup ice

Place all ingredients in a high-speed blender and blend for 1 minute until completely smooth.

MOOD ENHANCING BREW

At first glance, this may look like a regular old cup of hot cocoa with some strange ingredients added to it. And, in a way, I suppose that's what it is—but it's also a near-magical (and delicious) drink loaded with ingredients that can boost your mood, help keep stress levels in check, and create an all-around feeling of well-being. How? For one thing, cocoa, the star of the show, is loaded with essential and trace minerals (especially magnesium and valeric acid) that can help balance stress and mood swings.

Plus it contains PEA (or phenethylamine), which triggers the release of endorphins and mood-enhancing neurochemicals in the brain. In addition, maca, reishi, and ashwagandha, powerful adaptogens, are there to help create balance and calm. Adaptogens are a class of super-herbs and super-mushrooms named for their ability to help the body adapt to stress by regulating cortisol levels. Cortisol is our body's stress hormone. It essentially puts us into survival mode when we encounter a "fight or flight" situation. And because adaptogens naturally help guide our body to balance cortisol levels, we are likely to encounter a lift in mood and energy when we consume them. So, if you're a person who feels tired frequently and experiences a lot of stress, this delicious, restorative brew just might turn that frown upside down and, perhaps, even bring you to a place of calm.

Makes 1 serving

1 cup almond milk, or any milk you like

1 tablespoon coconut oil

1 tablespoon unsweetened cocoa powder or raw cacao powder

¼ to ½ teaspoon adaptogens of your choice, such as ashwagandha, reishi, or maca

2 tablespoons honey or maple syrup, or to taste

⅛ teaspoon cinnamon

Whisk together all ingredients in a medium saucepan set over medium heat. Cook until steaming, stirring occasionally. Serve immediately.

Note: Any time you consider taking something new to support a medical or health condition, check with your doctor, especially if you are pregnant or have an autoimmune issue.

BACK SOOTHING BALM ⌐

Back pain is unbelievably common. So common, in fact, that the average adult experiences it one to two times per year. It can be a recurring issue that gets triggered by all sorts of things, and the older we get, seemingly, the less it takes to bring on an "episode." I threw my back out a couple of years ago while putting my daughter's hair in a ponytail! Fortunately, most back pain isn't serious and resolves itself in a matter of weeks, but that doesn't mean it's fun to deal with in the meantime. Applying a homemade salve like this one can offer relief while spasms and strains heal. It's made with a hefty dose of cayenne, which works to reduce inflammation and relax muscles. The capsaicin in the pepper not only increases circulation, helping to reduce inflammation, but it also temporarily blocks nerve signals that communicate pain to the brain. So, when the balm is applied to the affected area, you'll initially feel warmth and then . . . nothing! You'll be somewhat numb.

Just bear in mind this stuff is hot! Don't use it on broken skin, open wounds, or near your eyes.

Makes about 4 ounces

¼ cup cayenne pepper

½ cup sunflower, almond, or olive oil

2 tablespoons beeswax pellets

1. In a blender or food processor, combine the cayenne and oil. Process for 30 seconds, until smooth and combined.

2. Pour the mixture into a clean, glass jar with a lid. Cover and store away from direct sunlight, shaking it daily, for 2 weeks.

3. Line a fine-mesh sieve with a few layers of cheesecloth, linen, or an old T-shirt and place over a clean bowl or jar. Pour the cayenne oil through the cheesecloth, squeezing the cloth to extract as much oil as possible. Discard the spent cayenne.

4. Gently melt the beeswax over low heat in a small sauce-pan. Stir in the cayenne oil until thoroughly combined. Pour the mixture into jars or tins and allow to cool. Store it in a cool dark place for up to 9 months.

5. To use: Scoop out a small amount of salve and slowly massage it into the affected area.

SORE MUSCLE RUB ✎

Being a human on this planet—just *being*—is hard on the body. Sitting for too long or staring at a computer screen is rough on our necks and shoulders. Running around after kids can be a killer on our backs. Exercising too much, not exercising enough . . . unless we hit an absolutely perfect equilibrium of fitness, nutrition, posture, and stress management, we're all pretty likely to have some minor aches and pains to contend with here and there. To deal with my occasional (OK, chronic) neck and back pain, I made this homemade muscle rub.

Cinnamon, clove, and cayenne—in the form of red pepper flakes here—give it a soothing, warming sensation and peppermint and eucalyptus create a refreshing, cooling sensation. It's perfect for easing tense muscles, reducing stiffness, and generally melting away discomfort. You gonna tell me you couldn't go for some of that? I thought not.

Makes about ¼ cup

¼ cup olive oil

2 teaspoons red pepper flakes

1 tablespoon beeswax pellets

10 drops peppermint essential oil

10 drops lavender essential oil

10 drops eucalyptus essential oil

5 drops cinnamon essential oil

5 drops clove essential oil

1. In a small pot set over low, warm the olive oil. Add the red pepper flakes and continue to heat for 30 minutes, until the oil becomes fragrant and takes on a reddish hue.

2. Strain the oil through a fine-mesh sieve or cheesecloth. Discard the red pepper flakes.

3. Place the infused olive oil and beeswax in a small heat-safe bowl or mason jar and place in a small saucepan filled with water over medium-low heat, stirring until the mixture is completely melted. Remove from the heat.

4. Add in the essential oils, then transfer to glass jars or tins and immediately cover.

5. Cool completely and cover. Store in a cool dark place.

6. To use: Rub into sore muscles liberally. Avoid using near eyes and make sure to wash your hands well after use.

WARMING RELIEF
FOR COLD FEET 🌶

Love is letting your spouse put their ice-cold feet on you in bed. This I know for sure. Well, my husband knows it. My feet are perpetually cold and he often finds them burrowing into his legs at night, *brrrr* . . . . But that's in the privacy of our own home. I can't reasonably expect him to keep my feet warm 100 percent of the time! And sometimes wooly socks, fluffy slippers, and even snow boots just don't cut it. So, what does? Cayenne! Makes sense when you think about it. I mean, what's more synonymous with "heat" than hot pepper? A bit sprinkled into a pair of socks is amazingly warming.

Just be sure your feet are free of any cuts, cracked heels, and basically any open skin before you give this remedy a go or you'll be in for some major *ouch*!

Makes 1 treatment

1 teaspoon cayenne pepper   1 pair cotton socks

1. Sprinkle ½ teaspoon of cayenne in one of the socks. Scrunch the sock a bit to distribute the powder evenly before sliding your foot in for the day.

2. Repeat with the second sock.

CLUSTER HEADACHE RELIEF 🌶

If you suffer from cluster headaches, chances are you're willing to try pretty much anything to stop getting those debilitating attacks. And who could blame you? Multiple, severe headaches that occur over the course of hours or days? Not cute. So what if I told you that shoving cayenne pepper up your nose might just be the answer you've been looking for? Nope, not kidding.

Intranasal capsaicin has been shown in multiple research studies to be effective in the treatment of cluster headaches. Researchers aren't 100 percent sure why it works, but the thought is that the capsaicin in cayenne peppers depletes nerves of a chemical called "Substance P," which sounds like something from a James Bond movie but is actually what our bodies produce to activate nerve fibers that cause swelling and pain in our sinus cavities and heads. When those fibers are turned off, they can't convey pain signals to the brain. So, applying capsaicin cream to the nostril has been shown to be an effective treatment.

Some people find immediate relief from swabbing their nostrils with capsaicin cream, while others have reported that it takes multiple applications to experience a reduction in severity and/or frequency of their headaches. Either way, know this: The capsaicin *will* cause a burning sensation in your nose that's likely to last for about 10 minutes. Unfortunately, for the treatment to be effective, this is one of those no-pain-no-gain scenarios. If you're lucky, the relief will be immediate—even if it isn't, the burning sensation should decrease with subsequent applications.

Makes about ⅓ cup

5 tablespoons coconut oil   1 tablespoon cayenne pepper

1. Heat the coconut oil in a small saucepan over medium heat or microwave on HIGH in 30-second spurts, until melted. Stir in the cayenne pepper.

2. Transfer the mixture to a clean jar, tin, or other lidded container and allow to cool. Cover and store away from direct sunlight for up to 6 months.

3. To use: Gently apply a small amount of cream to the nostril, using a cotton swab. For best results, use the cream on the same side as the headache.

RELIEF FOR NASAL CONGESTION 🌶

From allergies to colds to the flu, annoying and uncomfortable nasal congestion hits us all at one time or another. It's pretty much the *worst*. But before you reach for an over-the-counter decongestant—or maybe you already did and found that it either doesn't help or the side effects (dryness, restlessness, headache . . .) aren't worth it—give this natural decongestant a whirl. With plenty of cayenne to promote the flow of nasal secretions, this surprisingly tasty drink will really help clear out your nasal passages and provide relief. Honey, which not only tastes good, is there to help soothe and it also works as an antimicrobial to stomp out bacteria and viruses. And antiseptic apple cider vinegar helps stifle icky germs, too. All in all, it's a good way to stay hydrated when you're all stuffed up.

Makes 1 treatment

¾ cup hot water

2 tablespoons raw apple cider vinegar

1 tablespoon raw honey

⅛ to ¼ teaspoon cayenne pepper or more

Combine all ingredients in a mug. Stir and sip slowly.

SORE THROAT GARGLE

You've woken up with a sore throat. *Ruh roh.* Is this the first symptom of a cold, the flu, or—*gasp*—strep throat? Before you panic-run to the doctor's office or reach for a chemical-laden OTC medicine, consider trying this soothing gargle to treat the pain. Gargling is a simple and remarkably attractive—er, I mean *effective*—way to kill germs and soothe a sore throat. Cinnamon is packed with antiviral, antifungal, and antibacterial qualities that can soothe your sore throat. Cayenne's capsicum reduces inflammation and provides lasting pain relief (after the burn). Combine the two, and you're looking at a powerful potion for quick relief from throat pain and discomfort.

Makes 1 treatment

1 teaspoon ground cinnamon   1 cup warm water
1 teaspoon cayenne pepper

1. Combine cinnamon and cayenne in a glass with the warm water. Stir to combine.

2. Gargle with the solution two to three times a day.

Note: Less severe sore throats—those caused by environmental factors, allergies, or the common cold—should go away on their own in two or three days and can be assisted with at-home remedies. But if symptoms persist and you have a fever or show symptoms of white spots on your throat or tonsils, there may be something else going on that requires antibiotics or another form of doctor-directed treatment.

COCOA AND ORANGE COUGH DROPS 🍫

A few years ago, researchers at the University of Hull in England found that chocolate-based medicine worked better than cough syrup at treating nagging coughs. And if that doesn't sound like a made-up headline from *The Wonka Weekly News*, I don't know what does! But it's true: Researchers think chocolate may be the cure for persistent coughs. Well, sort of. In the study, researchers engaged more than 150 patients and found that those who took medicine containing cocoa got better more quickly than those who took regular cough syrup. Fine, they weren't exactly downing Snickers bars to cure their coughs. And it's unclear whether the alkaloid in cocoa is what helped relieve the inflammation and, therefore, quelled the coughs, or if, perhaps, it was the zinc that did the trick. Either way, the study proved what we chocolate lovers already knew: chocolate can fix just about anything. So, while you wait for cocoa cough medicine to hit the shelves, make these easy, all-natural, throat-soothing cough lozenges with cough-busting cocoa, antiseptic and antibacterial honey, a hit of vitamin C from the orange, and immune-boosting ginger.

Makes about 25 lozenges

2 tablespoons water

2 tablespoons raw honey

1 teaspoon cinnamon

½ teaspoon ground ginger

Grated zest from 1 orange

½ cup unsweetened cocoa powder

1. Combine water, honey, cinnamon, ginger, and orange zest in a medium bowl. Add ¼ cup of cocoa powder and stir to combine. Add the remaining cocoa powder 1 tablespoon at a time, blending well after each addition.

2. With cocoa-dusted hands, roll the dough into small balls about ½ inch in diameter and place on a parchment-lined sheet pan. Press dough balls with your fingers and flatten out until about ¼ inch thick.

3. Place lozenges on a baking sheet in the oven with the oven light on until they're completely dry, about 24 hours. Alternatively, you can dry them in a dehydrator by following the manufacturer's directions.

4. Store in an airtight container for up to 6 months.

DIGESTIVE AID 🌶

My stomach has become more and more finicky as I've aged, which, by the way, is pretty annoying for a person who has made a career of cooking and eating. I want to eat and drink what I want to eat and drink! Alas, some of the time my body (and my reflux) says otherwise. *Sigh* . . . . So, I'm forever on the hunt for ways to support my gut health and keep my digestion in check. And while it may seem counterintuitive to treat an already funky stomach with fiery cayenne, it can be incredibly effective.

Research suggests that consuming cayenne pepper stimulates our salivary glands, where digestion begins, and it also encourages the flow of enzyme production, an essential part of a healthy digestive system. It has also been shown to inhibit acid production naturally, which is welcome news for those of us who reluctantly rely on prescription or over-the-counter acid blockers to stop the pain and discomfort of acid reflux. So, if you were concerned that taking cayenne would cause heartburn, don't be. I drink this gut-loving tea often to keep my moody system happy. With cayenne, fresh ginger—well known for its stomach-soothing and digestion-supporting properties—and raw honey, with its laundry list of health benefits, this tea is hot and spicy but also soothing.

Makes 2 cups

½ teaspoon cayenne pepper

One 2-inch piece of fresh
  ginger, sliced thin

2 cups water

2 tablespoons raw honey,
  or to taste (optional)

1. Put cayenne, ginger, and water into a pot and bring to a boil. Reduce the heat and let simmer for 20 minutes. Stir in the honey, if using, and serve.

2. Sip slowly.

CONSTIPATION RELIEVER

"Gut health" has become part of mainstream medical and nutrition conversations of late. After all, colon health is important. The uncomfortable, painful feeling of being constipated is not fun. And while less frequent bowel movements or stools that are difficult to pass can come about from a variety of causes, it happens most often due to changes in diet or routine, or due to inadequate intake of fiber. Increasing dietary fiber, exercise, and liquids should help, but adding this cayenne remedy can also provide relief.

Cayenne, in small amounts, works really well to put a little giddy-up in the digestive system. It stimulates our taste buds, which in turn stimulates saliva production. As it moves down the digestive tract, cayenne stimulates the stomach to secrete hydrochloric acid, the pancreas to secrete enzymes into the small intestines, and the liver and gallbladder to secrete bile, all of which help digestion. It also triggers TRVP1 receptors, which detect and react to capsaicin (located in your mouth and also throughout your body and GI tract) and stimulate your GI tract—making things move. Fast.

One quick and easy way to treat constipation naturally is to down a glass of what is essentially spicy lemonade. Because citric acid, which is present in lemons, is a natural laxative and vitamin C softens the stool, lemon is a great partner for cayenne in treating occasional constipation.

Makes 1 treatment

1 teaspoon fresh lemon juice

1 cup warm water

⅛ to ¼ teaspoon
   cayenne pepper

Honey, to taste (optional)

1. Combine lemon juice, cayenne, water, and honey (if using) in a mug. Stir to combine.

2. Drink first thing in the morning before breakfast.

Note: If you have severe pain, blood in your stools, or constipation that lasts longer than three weeks, you should call your doctor.

METABOLISM BOOSTER 🌶

If there's one thing I've learned in the process of trying out natural healing and home remedies, it's that our bodies—while kind of weird—are also amazing. And so mysterious! Take metabolism, for example. Metabolism is the rate at which the body burns calories and converts what we eat and drink into energy. And while it most often comes up in the context of weight loss, "good" metabolism is mostly about properly breaking down your food and using it for overall health.

When it comes to making a lasting impact on our metabolic rate, there's really no magic bullet. Nothing works quite as well as eating good, *real* food, drinking plenty of water, exercising, and getting adequate sleep. And yet, try as we may, fitting all of that into every single day can be a tall order. For me, staying hydrated is one of the hardest parts. And it's one of the most important pieces of metabolism, too, especially when it comes to critical organs like the brain and heart. So I turn to water with cayenne and other beneficial ingredients for a little extra help. It's a tried-and-true way to help our body's metabolism run smoothly.

Studies have shown that cayenne can raise metabolic rates by as much as 25 percent and—bonus—can even help with fat loss. And because it's an overall stimulant, it encourages our cells to work more efficiently, improving not only blood circulation, but also our lymphatic health. This recipe not only includes a good dose of cayenne, but it also calls for 4 cups of water, which gets us well on our way to healthy hydration. Stir up a pitcher at night and down your first glass before breakfast the next morning to get the day started off right!

Makes about 4 cups

One 2- to 4-inch piece fresh ginger, or more to taste, sliced thin

1 stick cinnamon

1 tablespoon raw, unfiltered apple cider vinegar

¼ teaspoon cayenne pepper

4 cups water

½ lemon, juiced

1. Combine the ginger, cinnamon stick, apple cider vinegar, cayenne, and water in a jar or pitcher. Stir or shake to mix. Cover and refrigerate overnight.

2. In the morning, add the lemon juice and stir to combine.

3. Drink 1 to 4 cups daily.

HEALING TREATMENT FOR CUTS AND WOUNDS ✒

You're really going to think I'm off my rocker with this one, but cayenne pepper is a great thing to apply to cuts and scrapes. It's rich in vitamin K, the vitamin that facilitates the coagulation of the blood, so it can help stop the bleeding. Fast! I'm sure you're thinking what I originally thought when I learned about this remedy, which is, *Doesn't that hurt like mad?* Well, yeah it does. But, thanks to the pain-killing properties of cayenne, it actually helps relieve pain after a few minutes. And it doesn't *really* hurt that much more than whatever else you might rub on an open wound.

I keep a little container on hand in my first-aid kit in the car and one in a backpack when we go hiking. It's indispensable!

Of course, serious wounds require immediate medical attention, so if you've got a very deep cut and/or it won't stop bleeding after applying moderate pressure for several minutes, if the injured person has not had a tetanus shot within 5 to 10 years, or if the cut is from a human or animal bite, head straight to the emergency room.

Makes 1 treatment

A pinch to ⅛ teaspoon cayenne pepper, depending on the size of the cut

1. Gently wash the affected area with clean, warm water.

2. With *clean* hands, apply the cayenne to the affected area. Once you've covered the affected area, place a band-aid, rolled gauze, or gauze held in place with paper tape over the wound.

3. Change the dressing at least once a day until the wound is healed.

TOOTHACHE RELIEF 🌶

Whether from a cavity, a cracked tooth, or a loose filling, tooth-aches are pretty awful. And while persistent tooth pain should always be treated by a dental professional, a home remedy is an easy and inexpensive way to provide temporary relief while you wait for minor pain to resolve itself or until you can get on your dentist's calendar. Here, capsaicin works its magic, blocking the pain signals to the brain and reducing inflammation. Antibacterial ginger helps fight off infection, which is especially helpful if you've got an abscess; it also helps keep swelling at bay. Since this concoction is pretty spicy, I wouldn't rush to use it with children, but most adults and teens should be able to tolerate the cotton long enough for the paste to work.

Makes 1 treatment

1 teaspoon cayenne pepper

1 teaspoon freshly grated ginger

1. Combine cayenne and ginger with enough water to form a paste. Dip a cotton ball into the mixture, making sure to saturate it completely.

2. Place the soaked cotton ball on the affected tooth, leaving it in place until the pain has reduced or (hopefully) subsided entirely. Repeat as necessary.

Note: Severe tooth pain should be treated by an emergency dentist as soon as possible, even if the home remedy provides pain relief.

POISON IVY REMEDY

This is an old recipe for something called Kloss' Liniment. It was developed in the 1800s by Jethro Kloss, a natural health enthusiast and herbalist who dedicated his life to caring for people. Never mind the fact that he had some ideas that didn't quite take off (kerosene for wound care being one of them), but this now-popular liniment is a strong and fantastic remedy to have on hand. It can be used for reducing muscle soreness, cleansing wounds, and soothing insect bites, but I've found it to be most helpful in treating poison ivy. Anti-inflammatory cayenne, antimicrobial myrrh, antibiotic echinacea, and goldenseal all help to reduce oozing, spreading, itching, and inflammation. It does require about a month of steeping, so I suggest making it in early spring so that it's ready when poison ivy starts to creep and crawl all over the place. All the ingredients can be found in either a well-stocked health food store or online.

Makes about 1 cup

2 tablespoons echinacea powder

2 tablespoons goldenseal

2 tablespoons myrrh powder

2 teaspoons cayenne powder

2 cups 70% rubbing alcohol

1. Combine the herbs and cayenne in a glass jar. Add the rubbing alcohol and cover with a tight-fitting lid.

2. Store the mixture at room temperature for 4 weeks.

3. Strain and decant into a clean jar or bottle.

ECLEMA TREATMENT

If you suffer from eczema, chances are you've spent a fair amount of time trying an array of treatments to deal with it. I imagine you've slathered, vacuumed, eaten, and soaked your way to . . . not much relief? Well, you're not alone. More than three million people suffer from eczema, an itchy, inflamed skin condition that can come about from a variety of causes, including atopic dermatitis, contact dermatitis, dyshidrotic eczema, nummular eczema, seborrheic dermatitis, and stasis dermatitis. Finding the root cause, be it genetics or environmental factors, can be the first step toward getting symptoms under control, but finding a treatment that makes you *feel* better is not always easy.

There are loads of eczema treatments on the market—both prescription and over-the-counter; finding what works for you takes some trial and error. However, if you're looking to give an all-natural treatment a try, this remedy is a good place to start. Cocoa butter is the superstar here; it's high in fatty acids so it hydrates and nourishes the skin, while forming a protective barrier to hold in moisture. Coconut oil provides additional hydration, while raw honey is not only anti-inflammatory, an antioxidant, and antimicrobial but also a powerful humectant. And lavender contributes antifungal properties and reduces inflammation. Plus, its soothing scent may be just what you need to calm your nerves if you're about ready to pull your hair out over this whole skin debacle!

Makes about 1 cup

½ cup cocoa butter

½ cup coconut oil

1 tablespoon raw honey

30 drops lavender essential oil

1. Place the cocoa butter and coconut oil in a small heat-safe bowl or mason jar and place in a small saucepan filled with water over medium-low heat, stirring until the mixture is completely melted.

2. Add the honey and continue to stir. Remove from the heat and add the lavender oil. Stir to combine. Set aside to cool for 5 to 10 minutes.

3. Using a handheld or a stand mixer, whip the mixture for 3 to 5 minutes, until frothy and smooth.

4. Transfer to a mason jar or other lidded container. Store at room temperature for up to 3 months.

SKIN SMOOTHING BEAUTY SHOT 🌶

We all know that there's no such thing as a magic potion. Just ask Alice from *Alice in Wonderland*. Oh. Actually . . . bad example. Well, in *real* life, there is no one pill or drink, no lotion or potion, that can magically change the way we look or feel. However, when it comes to having a healthy complexion, while diet and lifestyle make the greatest difference, there are a few little helpers we can count on to give our skin a boost. This little green shot is chock-full of skin-loving nutrients that will brighten and smooth your skin from the inside out. Spirulina, a type of blue-green algae (yes, that's why this shot looks a teensy bit like something the Loch Ness Monster might order at happy hour), is a fantastic source of beta-carotene, which is amazing for your skin. It keeps collagen fibers intact, promoting smoother, firmer skin. Cucumber contains a good dose of silica, which also helps with collagen production. And cayenne helps with inflammation and increases blood flow to the skin, bringing with it oxygen and antioxidants, all of which promote cell turnover. Apple juice is there mostly because it tastes good, but apples are high in vitamin C, which is great for supporting collagen production. Shoot back this beauty shot once a day and look forward to healthy, radiant skin.

Makes 2 servings

¼ teaspoon spirulina

⅛ to ¼ teaspoon
   cayenne pepper

2 tablespoons cucumber
   juice (see note)

¼ cup apple juice

Combine all ingredients in a small bowl, stir to combine, then pour into two shot glasses and drink. Alternatively, you can add the ingredients to a cocktail shaker filled with ice, shake until chilled, then pour into shot glasses and drink.

Note: If you don't have a juicer, you can easily make cucumber juice as follows:

Peel 1 or 2 cucumbers, cut off the ends, and roughly chop. Set a strainer lined with cheesecloth, a thin dish towel, or a coffee filter over a medium bowl. Process the cucumbers in a food processor or blender until they resemble, well, mush. Alternatively, you can grate them on a box grater. Pour the pulverized cucumbers into the strainer and, using a spatula or large spoon, press the pulp to extract the juice. Compost the pulp or reserve for another purpose. Store the juice in the refrigerator for up to a week.

BEAUTY
SECRETS

MOISTURIZING CHOCOLATE-COCONUT FACE MASK

I'll confess that in recent years I haven't been great about making time to use face masks. It seems like just one more step in an already jam-packed day. And sometimes one more step is more than I can handle. Really. Life can be overwhelming, and the little things add up. I don't know what you've been through lately, but I've had *a year*. It's made me crave simplicity more than ever. But I've also realized that, even amid all the crazy, making time to do little things for myself is important. And so, I've resolved to make skin care a priority. Simple skin care, like this ridiculously easy, two-ingredient mask, made with little more than cocoa powder and coconut oil.

Cocoa powder, with its boatload of antioxidants, vitamins, and minerals, promotes cell repair, helps firm skin, and prevents wrinkles. Coconut oil is anti-inflammatory and provides long-lasting moisture that, amazingly, doesn't feel greasy. Use this mask when you can. Even if it means putting off being "productive." Sometimes, even when life is a lot, we've got to put our best face forward, and if a healthy complexion helps you do that, then it's most certainly worth your while.

Makes 1 treatment

1 tablespoon coconut oil

2 tablespoons unsweetened dark cocoa powder

1. Spoon coconut oil into a small microwave-safe bowl. Microwave on HIGH 10 to 15 seconds, until it has begun to soften.

2. Add the cocoa powder to the coconut oil and stir until smooth.

3. To use: Apply the mixture to a just-cleaned face, avoiding the eye area. Relax for 15 to 20 minutes, then rinse with warm water.

ACNE-FIGHTING AVOCADO FACE MASK

There are lots of reasons acne might dare to show its face . . . on your face. Excess oil production, clogged pores, bacteria, and inflammation are among the likely culprits. But stress, poor diet, too much alcohol, and hormonal imbalances can all be to blame, too. There's no need to panic over those pimples. This powerful-yet-soothing mask can set you on your way to a clearer complexion.

Cayenne, with its powerful anti-inflammatory properties, increases blood flow and circulation, thereby helping to fight off breakouts. Cocoa powder is a rich source of sulfur, which reduces oily skin and prevents pore blockage, plus it contains copper, zinc, iron, and magnesium, all of which stimulate tissue repair and cell growth. And moisturizing and soothing avocado has anti-inflammatory effects, which can help to keep acne-related redness and inflammation at bay. And despite what your intuition may be telling you about putting something as high in fat as avocado on your oily or acne-prone face, moisturizing is key to keeping all skin healthy. Avocado hydrates without leaving an oily mess. So, get ready to zap those zits with this quick and easy mask.

Makes 1 treatment

½ ripe avocado

1 teaspoon cayenne pepper

1 teaspoon unsweetened
cocoa powder

1. Place avocado in a small bowl. Mash with a fork until smooth. Add the cayenne and cocoa and mix to combine.

2. Apply the mixture to a just-cleaned face, avoiding the eye area. Relax for 20 minutes, then rinse with warm water.

COCOA BUTTER
EYE CREAM

Is anyone else *so over* our culture's never-ending obsession with clinging to youth? My social media feed is full of ads for serums, oils, treatments, injections, and *procedures* to convince me that I need to look younger, longer. But "younger" is not better. Truly, it isn't. There is such beauty in aging. There is wisdom, grace, and character—visible character—that comes from having lived life. I try to remember this, even as the creep of age has begun to show on my face. There are creases here and there, "fine lines" around my eyes, and signs of gravity winning out. But I don't buy anti-aging products, because I'm not interested in fighting it. I'm interested in aging well. And to that end, I eat a reasonably healthy diet with enough indulgences to keep me happy, exercise to maintain my energy and flexibility, wear what I like wearing, and use products that make me feel good. That includes cleansing, moisturizing, and using sunscreen on my face—because taking care of my skin, including the fragile skin under my eyes, makes me feel good. That skin is the thinnest on the entire body, which is why it's prone to dark circles, bags, wrinkles, and puffiness; therefore, it requires a bit of special care.

Regular moisturizers can be harsh and irritating to the skin around the eyes, so I use this gentle but highly effective homemade eye cream. With cocoa butter—rich in omega-3, omega-6, vitamin E, and vitamin K—and coconut oil, an excellent source of lauric acid and essential fats, this eye cream softens and protects delicate skin and keeps connective tissue strong and supple. Let's all slap on a bit of eye cream, remember to never neglect ourselves, and—hard as it sometimes is to do—be grateful for the chance to get older.

Makes about ¼ cup

1 tablespoon cocoa butter

2 tablespoons coconut oil

1 tablespoon beeswax pellets

½ teaspoon vitamin E oil

1. Place the cocoa butter, coconut oil, and beeswax in a small heat-safe bowl or mason jar, and place in a small saucepan filled with water over medium-low heat, stirring until the mixture is completely melted. Remove from the heat and allow the mixture to cool for 15 minutes.

2. Add the vitamin E oil and, using a whisk or immersion blender, whip the mixture until the vitamin E is thoroughly incorporated.

3. Transfer the eye cream to a lidded container and store at room temperature for up to 3 months.

4. To use: Gently massage or tap a pea-sized amount of eye cream into the area below your eyes using your ring or middle finger. Start in the innermost corner and move outward, avoiding your bottom eyelashes.

COCOA BODY SCRUB

Can somebody please explain to me why kids, at a certain age, start to hate taking showers? I don't get it—showers are the *best*! I've tried a lot of gimmicks to make showering fun: I've made bath paints, soap slime, and sometimes I even let them take disco showers with loud music, lights off, and glow sticks. Sometimes I just yell. That's not as fun . . .

But here's something that makes showering enjoyable for all: a delicious, almost-good-enough-to-eat chocolate-y body scrub. It's gently exfoliating, incredibly moisturizing, and intoxicatingly scented. I like it just as it is, with its pure chocolate aroma, but you can customize it with a variety of essential oils to change things up. I make a version for my kids that I call "mint chip," which is the recipe below with the addition of peppermint oil. You could make yours chocolate-orange, chocolate-raspberry, or whatever scent combo works for you. This also makes a really great gift, spooned into cute little jars and tied with some bakers' twine or pretty ribbon.

Makes about 1 cup

½ cup brown sugar

3 tablespoons unsweetened cocoa powder

2 tablespoons cocoa butter, melted

¼ cup sweet almond oil or olive oil

10 to 20 drops essential oil, such as peppermint, orange, or raspberry (optional)

1. Combine sugar, cocoa powder, melted cocoa butter, almond oil, and essential oil, if using, in a small bowl. Stir to combine.

2. Store in an airtight container.

3. To use: Apply to wet skin. Scrub in a circular motion. Rinse.

COCOA MINT SOAP

If you've thumbed through my book, *The Olive Oil & Sea Salt Companion* (and I *certainly* hope you have), you already know all about my stubborn refusal to make my own soap. From scratch, anyway. Soap-making typically requires the use of some strong chemicals and harder-to-source ingredients and, somewhere along the line, I declared myself to be Someone Who Doesn't Make Soap. But there's a loophole in my obstinance and that is a pre-made base. Soap base is simply pre-made soap you can melt down and customize in tons of ways. You control the fragrance, color, texture, and shape without having to handle any caustic chemicals or wear much in the way of safety gear. Soap bases are available at most craft stores and lots of websites. One of my absolute favorite semi-homemade soap recipes is this one, which is evocative of mint chip ice cream. It uses a shea butter base, which gives it an opaque look and creamy consistency. Goat's milk soap is a good substitute if you can't find shea butter, but any opaque base will work. I love to give this soap as gifts—especially on Valentine's Day—when the mixture can be poured into candy molds and packaged like a box of chocolates. (Just be sure your recipient knows they aren't edible!)

Makes about 6 bars of soap, depending on the size

- 1 pound shea butter soap base, cut into cubes
- 2 tablespoons unsweetened natural cocoa powder
- 2 tablespoons chopped fresh mint or 1 teaspoon dried mint
- 5 to 10 drops peppermint essential oil

1. Place the soap base in a large microwave-safe bowl and microwave on HIGH in 30-second intervals until melted, stirring after each interval.

2. Add the cocoa powder, mint, and peppermint essential oil. Stir until combined.

3. Pour the mixture into a silicone soap mold, a loaf pan lined with parchment, or an empty ½ gallon milk carton with one side cut off. Set aside for about an hour, until firm.

4. Unmold the soap and, using a sharp knife, bench scraper, or wire clay cutter, slice the soap into bars.

COCOA BODY BUTTER

When I was pregnant with my first kid, I heard that cocoa butter supposedly prevented stretch marks. I researched it, bought some, and got ready to start applying it all over my bump. In doing so, I learned three things: 1) Nothing "erases" stretch marks, although keeping skin well-hydrated might be some help in preventing them; 2) My belly is more prone to becoming crazy itchy during pregnancy than ending up with stretch marks; and 3) Cocoa butter doesn't slather at all! It's as solid as a bar of soap and not at all easy to spread on skin.

But here I was with all this cocoa butter and I was determined to find a way to use it. This luxurious, delicious body butter is the result of that determination. With only two ingredients—emollient rich cocoa butter and sweet almond oil—this happy accident is incredibly fluffy, intoxicatingly chocolate-y, and, to this day, one of my favorite mainstays in the bathroom cabinet. It's almost shockingly easy to make and even more astonishing how velvety and not-greasy it leaves your skin.

Makes about 1½ cups

¾ cup cocoa butter

¼ cup sweet almond oil (may substitute olive, coconut, or avocado oil)

1. Place the cocoa butter and almond oil in a small heat-safe bowl or mason jar. Put bowl or jar in a small saucepan filled with water over medium-low heat, stirring until the mixture is completely melted.

2. Transfer the mixture to a medium bowl and refrigerate for 30 minutes.

3. Using a handheld electric mixer or a stand mixer, whip the cocoa butter and almond oil for 5 minutes, until light and fluffy.

4. Transfer your body butter to a jar or tin. Store at room temperature for up to 3 months.

5. To use: Slather it on!

AFTER-SUN MOISTURIZER

Once upon a time in a haze of naivete and vanity (otherwise known as my teenage years), I would slick myself in a generous coating of baby oil and literally bake my skin in the sun for *hours*. And, somehow, I never once got a sunburn. How?! It wasn't until my late 20s, when I was on vacation in a country much closer to the equator than the northeastern United States, that I experienced my first burn and—holy smokes— was I in for a wakeup call. After that, I acquainted myself with the concept of SPF and started to take care to wear hats, reapply sunscreen, and generally start acting like a grownup in the sun. That said, no one's perfect. I've definitely had some slipups here and there, resulting in the occasional burn. And what I've found is that one of the best ways to give some soothing love to painful, sunburned skin is with this balm, which contains pretty much every ingredient I can think of to soothe and heal sunburned skin.

Cocoa butter is the unequivocal star, as it is well known to rejuvenate, moisturize, and nourish damaged skin cells, but I've thrown in vitamin E, aloe vera gel, raw honey, and coconut oil to cover all the soothing skin bases here. Even if you don't have a sunburn but have spent a day in the sun, this moisturizer works beautifully to keep skin soft and hydrated.

Makes about 1 cup

¼ cup cocoa butter

1 tablespoon coconut oil

¼ cup beeswax

2 tablespoons aloe vera gel

2 tablespoons raw honey

1 teaspoon vitamin E oil

1. Place the cocoa butter, coconut oil, and beeswax in a small heat-safe bowl or mason jar. Put the bowl or jar in a small saucepan filled with water over medium-low heat, stirring until the mixture is completely melted. Remove from the heat and allow the mixture to cool for 15 minutes.

2. Add the aloe vera, honey, and vitamin E and stir to combine.

3. Transfer your moisturizer to a jar or tin (or several, if you prefer). Store at room temperature for up to 3 months.

4. To use: Gently slather onto just-cleaned, towel-dried skin after sun exposure.

DIY BRONZING LOTION

Let's be honest: Getting a little sun on your face looks great. But, alas, we know that's ill advised. Thankfully, you can get that perfectly sun-kissed look without any actual sun if you find the right bronzer. Even better? You can make your own with a handful of ingredients you likely already have in your kitchen and bathroom. Because you're in control of everything that goes into this bronzer (unlike expensive products from the makeup counter), you can whip up the *exact* right shade for your complexion.

Play around with the ratio of cocoa and cornstarch to alter how deeply hued your bronzer is, and add more or less cinnamon to control the tone's warmth. (More cinnamon = a warmer color.) If you like, you can even add a bit of bronze mica powder for a bit of shimmer. I usually skip that ingredient, as I always feel like a walking disco ball when I wear shimmer, but if a little sparkle is your thing, you should absolutely add it for some extra glow. Either way, when you swipe on this creamy chocolate bronzer, you'll instantly look like you spent a week on an island—without the burn. Or tan lines.

Makes about 2 tablespoons

1 to 2 teaspoons
unsweetened natural
cocoa powder

¼ to ½ teaspoon cinnamon

1 to 2 teaspoons cornstarch
powder, if you want
a lighter-toned bronzer

1 tablespoon face lotion
of your choice, or
more as desired

½ teaspoon coconut oil or
cocoa butter, melted
and cooled slightly

1. Combine all the ingredients in a small bowl, stirring well to combine.

2. Test the color on the back of your hand or on the inside of your wrist, adjusting ingredients until you're happy with the color and you achieve an easily spreadable consistency.

3. Store in an airtight container at room temperature for up to 6 months.

4. To use: Swipe the bronzing cream onto your face any- where you'd like to look like you've gotten a bit of sun, such as your forehead, cheekbones, the bridge of your nose, and along your jawline. Use your fingers or a makeup brush to blend.

NATURAL COLOR-DEPOSITING CONDITIONER FOR BRUNETTES

If you color your hair, no matter how well you care for it, the color eventually fades. You can, however, use a color-depositing conditioner to keep it from looking lackluster and otherwise spent. This is not news: Color-depositing conditioners have been around for a long time. But I bet you didn't know that you could make it yourself. Yes, you can, and it's an incredibly easy, quick, and a virtually foolproof way to keep your color looking great. Because color conditioner is more or less a "regular" conditioner with pigment added to it, making your own is simply a matter of finding the right hue to add to your favorite conditioner.

Lots of ingredients can be used in DIY color conditioners—from beets to carrots, lemon to sage—but one of the best for brown hair is cocoa powder. On its own, cocoa deepens dark tones in light and medium brown hair, although it can be used on lighter shades to add depth or lowlights. Cocoa can also be mixed with coffee or cinnamon to create a range of colors from cool brown to chestnut or mahogany. It's fun to play around and find a shade that suits you best. I've given you a base recipe below, but feel free to concoct until you achieve a color that works. The longer you leave it in your hair, the deeper the color. In general, though, you'll use this as you would any other conditioner. In fact, you can swap your homemade color conditioner for your usual conditioner a few times per week or whenever your tone needs a little pep.

Makes about 1 cup

½ cup good-quality   2 heaping tablespoons
   hair conditioner   natural cocoa powder

1. Combine conditioner and cocoa powder in a medium bowl.
   Stir well to incorporate.

2. To use: Apply generously to wet hair. Leave on for 2 to
   5 minutes. Rinse thoroughly. Style as usual.

DRY SHAMPOO

Dry shampoo is a pretty genius idea. For the uninitiated, dry shampoo is a powder that provides a water-free way of cleaning your hair. It absorbs excess sebum and other oils from your roots and generally freshens up your locks. It's an amazing way to buy yourself some extra sleep in the morning, preserve hair color, freshen up after workouts, or make a blowout last an extra day or two. But for the longest time, I thought I wasn't a good candidate for dry shampoo, because my hair color is really dark and lots of dry shampoos are made of some kind of white powder. While those helped absorb oil, I was left with what looked like a world-class case of dandruff. Ew. That is, until I crawled out from under my rock and discovered that, duh, some dry shampoo comes in shades that match hair color in order to avoid exactly that problem. So, that was on the upside, but the other discoveries I made were that—holy cow—dry shampoo is expensive! And full of weird chemicals! And by weird I mean, stuff like phenoxyethanol and hydroxypropyltrimonium. Do *you* know what hydroxypropyltrimonium is?! I don't, but I'm pretty sure I don't want to breathe it in after spraying it around my head. Not only is this homemade dry shampoo free of any unpronounceable chemicals, it can be customized to match your hair color and it smells fantastic. Below is the formula I use for my dark brown hair, but I've provided a bit of a cheat sheet for other hair colors in the notes below.

Makes 3 to 4 uses

½ cup unsweetened cocoa powder (and/or some activated charcoal, cinnamon, or cornstarch, depending on the shade you hope to achieve; see below)

2 tablespoons baking soda

1. Combine cocoa powder or cornstarch (or a combination of the two), cinnamon or charcoal (if using), and baking soda in a small glass jar, ideally with a shaker top.

2. To use: Sprinkle a small amount on your hair just at the scalp area. Allow the powder to absorb the dirt and oils for a minute or two, then flip your hair upside down, use your fingers to blend the powder, shake out your roots, and allow the dry shampoo to move toward your ends. Give your hair a quick brush, then hit the road.

HOW TO CUSTOMIZE DRY SHAMPOO TO SUIT YOUR HAIR COLOR

For very dark brown or black hair, swap out some or all of the cocoa powder for activated charcoal.

For auburn hair, swap out some of the cocoa powder for cinnamon.

For red hair, swap out all the cocoa powder for cinnamon.

For medium and light brown hair, use a combination of cocoa powder and cornstarch.

For dark blonde hair, use mostly cornstarch with just a bit of cocoa powder to match your roots.

SHINE BOOSTING HAIR MASK 🌶

From cold weather to heat styling and everything in between, our hair goes through a lot that can leave it dry, damaged, and dull. But I've got a great solution! A simple combination of cayenne pepper and olive oil is all it takes to enhance your hair's natural brilliance and nourish it from roots to ends. By helping to stimulate blood circulation to the scalp, cayenne pepper adds vitality to dull, lifeless hair and—according to research—may even stimulate hair growth. Olive oil, rich in healthy fats and vitamin E, helps to repair damage that causes breakage and split ends and makes the hair look shiny and sleek. Use this treatment weekly and your hair will be healthier and shinier with less frizz and fewer split ends.

Makes about 2 cups

2 tablespoons cayenne pepper

2 cups extra virgin olive oil

1. Combine cayenne pepper and extra virgin olive oil in a jar or bottle and allow the mixture to steep, away from direct sunlight, for about two weeks.

2. To use: Section your hair and apply the treatment generously to damp or dry hair from roots to ends. Massage the product into your scalp. Cover your hair with a shower cap and/or a warm towel. Leave the oil on for 30 to 60 minutes before washing your hair with shampoo and conditioner.

HOT COCOA BATH SOAK

How often have you been in the middle of enjoying something delicious and actually said aloud, "This is so good I could literally take a bath in it"? Well, if that something was of the rich and chocolatey variety, then here's your *literal* chance. This hot cocoa bath soak is so easy to make, with ingredients you probably already have around, that your bathing-in-chocolate dreams can come true as soon as right now. With a decadent combination of ingredients that soften, smooth, detoxify, and pamper the skin, this is just the thing to keep on hand when nothing but chocolate will cure what ails you. We've all been there! It also makes an absolutely adorable gift, packed into little mason jars or—even cuter—mini milk bottles.

Makes about 5 cups, about 10 uses

1 cup Epsom salts

1 cup coarse sea salt

¼ cup unsweetened cocoa powder

2 cups confectioners' sugar

½ cup cornstarch

½ cup baking soda

1. In a medium bowl, combine all the ingredients and mix well.

2. Transfer to an airtight container and store in a cool dry place.

3. To use: Add ½ cup to warm bath water. Swirl it around the water to mix it in. Relax and enjoy.

PLUMPING LIP STAIN

I happen to be a big fan of bright, bold lipstick. On days when I've managed to find time for a workout but can't quite squeeze in a shower until evening (*shhh . . . don't tell*), I give my lips a swipe of red and suddenly look put together enough to run a few errands and show my face at school pickup. But whether I'm rocking a bright lip or going for a more neutral tone, I want my kisser to look full and like there's something *there*, you know? This lip stain is my secret to smooth, moisturized, fuller looking lips. And not only does it make my pout look and feel great, it's also a fantastic way to use up that little bit of lipstick left at the end of the tube. With cocoa butter for moisture and both cinnamon and cayenne to increase blood flow and plump lips, this tinted, tingly stain can be used on its own or under your favorite lipstick.

Makes about 1 tablespoon

1 tablespoon cocoa butter or coconut oil, melted

1 teaspoon olive oil

¼ to ½ teaspoon lipstick (1 or more colors)

¼ teaspoon food-grade cinnamon essential oil

¼ teaspoon cayenne pepper

1. Combine melted cocoa butter, olive oil, lipstick, cinnamon oil, and cayenne in a small bowl. Stir to combine. Set aside to cool.

2. To use: Once cooled, apply a small amount of the lip stain directly to your lips, gently massaging in a circular motion. Wear alone or follow with your favorite lipstick.

3. Store remaining lip stain at room temperature in a small airtight container with a tight-fitting lid.

LIP BALM 🌰

I would argue that lip balm is a necessity for everyone. Regardless of age, season, or climate, all of us must contend with dry, flaky, or chapped lips at one point or another. And while just about any lip balm will help problem-solve, if your pucker is especially parched, you're going to want to have this recipe in your arsenal. Not only does it contain cocoa butter—one of the best hydrating ingredients out there—it also uses coconut oil for added moisture, honey for a touch of sweetness and healing properties, and cocoa powder because . . . well, if any old lip balm is good, isn't chocolate lip balm better? This balm will banish flakes and moisturize your lips with all-natural ingredients that you can feel great about (and pronounce). And better yet—it takes just 15 minutes to make and less than a half hour to set before it's ready to use.

Makes 10 to 12 pots or tubes

2 tablespoons coconut oil	1 teaspoon honey
1 tablespoon beeswax pellets	1 teaspoon cocoa powder
2 tablespoons cocoa butter	Lip balm tubes or tins

1. Place the coconut oil, beeswax, and cocoa butter in a small heat-safe bowl or mason jar, and place it in a small saucepan filled with water over medium-low heat, stirring until the mixture is completely melted. Add the honey and cocoa powder and stir to combine.

2. Remove from the heat, then carefully pour into tubes or tins and let set for 20 to 30 minutes.

3. Store in a cool dry place.

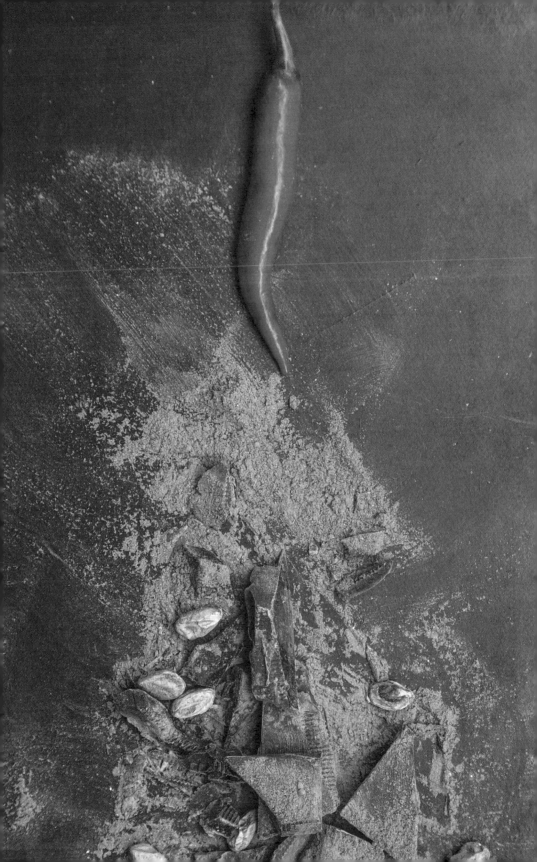

AROUND THE HOME

COCOA CANDLES

Making cocoa butter candles is a fun little project that offers serious reward with very little effort. We're talking melt, pour, done. Truly, it's just about the easiest DIY craft ever. Not only that, they burn slow and clean (unlike paraffin candles that release carcinogens into the air) and scent the air with the cozy, intoxicating aroma of chocolate. I love to make a bunch of these and keep them on hand to bring as host/hostess gifts. Of course, they also make lovely holiday presents and are even a fun thing to give as party favors. While jars work beautifully, they're adorable poured into vintage teacups, old crocks, and even painted tin cans. Really, any heat-proof container will work. The sky's the limit!

Makes 2 to 6 candles, depending on the size of your jars

Wick stickers, hot glue, or tape

Medium cotton wicks, with wick tabs attached (can be purchased online or at your local craft store)

Jars, tins, or other non-flammable containers, anywhere from 4 to 12 ounces

1 pound beeswax, pellets, or solid beeswax, cut into small pieces

1 cup cocoa butter, melted

1 tablespoon unsweetened cocoa powder

Continued

1. Prepare your containers by adding a wick sticker, dab of hot glue, or piece of tape onto the bottom of the wick tab and press them firmly inside the bottoms of your jars or tins.

2. Melt the wax and cocoa butter in a double boiler. (If you don't have a double boiler, place an inch of water in a saucepan, then place a smaller pot or stainless steel bowl inside, and bring the water to a low simmer.) Stir in the cocoa powder.

3. When the mixture is completely melted, *carefully* pour the hot wax into containers. Set the wicks so that they're centered, then lay a pencil or chopstick across the jars and tape the wicks to them.

4. Place the candles in a warm place, like your oven (set it to WARM or 170°F while you're making the candles, then turn it off before placing the candles inside), to harden slowly. If they cool too quickly, the wax can crack.

5. Allow the candles to cure for 48 hours, then trim the wicks to about ¼ inch.

PREVENTION FOR BOAT BARNACLES

Boat owners, it seems, will try almost anything to keep their crafts' undersides from attracting barnacles, those small, shelled sea creatures that can be found basically cemented to the bottoms of boats, on rocks, shells, and other underwater surfaces. In addition to being unsightly, barnacles can damage boats, so boaters are right to worry. To keep them away, the undersides of boats are often coated in something called antifouling paint that kills barnacle larvae. Unfortunately, the active ingredients in these treatments can get into the water and kill other kinds of marine life, too. One old-fashioned remedy is to mix loads of cayenne pepper with paint and to coat the bottom of the boat with the mixture. I don't own a boat, but if I did, I would certainly give this a try. And then I would name my boat The Barnacle Babe. No, better! If I ever start a band we will specialize in yacht rock and will be called Barnacle Babe and the Red Hot Peppers. (I'll probably keep my day job.)

Makes about 1 gallon

1 gallon exterior paint (does not have to be marine paint, as this will go on as a final coating)

3 cups cayenne pepper

1. In a large bucket, add paint and cayenne and stir well.

2. Using a roller or brush, paint the mixture onto your primed or painted (and dry) boat bottom. Repeat as necessary. Allow paint to dry thoroughly between coats.

SPOON BUTTER 🫘

If you're a fan of wooden kitchen tools, as I am, then you may already know what spoon butter is. If not and you were hoping that it was some kind of delicious buttery treat to be eaten with a spoon, I'm sorry to disappoint. (And if you thought it was butter made from spoons, I'm not quite sure how to help you, friend.) Spoon butter is simply a mixture of oil and beeswax used to moisturize and protect wooden boards, spoons, and utensil handles. It prolongs the lifespan of wooden kitchen tools and prevents cracking and splitting. You can purchase premade spoon butter; however, I much prefer to make my own with a combination of cocoa butter, coconut oil, and beeswax. It gives a gorgeous luminosity to treated wood and—bonus—it moisturizes and softens your hands while you use it!

Makes about ¼ cup

2 tablespoons cocoa butter
4 tablespoons coconut oil

2 tablespoons beeswax pellets

1. Place the cocoa butter, coconut oil, and beeswax in a small heat-safe bowl or mason jar and place in a small saucepan filled with water over medium-low heat, stirring until the mixture is completely melted. Remove from the heat and allow the mixture to cool for 15 minutes.

2. Once cool, apply a generous layer to your wooden items. Rub the spoon butter into the wood and let it sit for several hours or overnight to give it a chance to soak in. When most of the spoon butter is absorbed, use a clean cloth to rub off any excess and return the items to normal use.

HOMEMADE CHOCOLATE PLAYDOUGH

I've always loved Play-Doh and am glad that my kids haven't completely outgrown it yet. It's great for creativity and fine motor skills, and there's something so satisfying about its rubbery squish! Making homemade playdough is really easy and I like it even better than buying it, because you can customize it in so many ways. In my house, we've done every color of the rainbow, scented our playdough, and even added glitter to it. But one of my kids' all-time favorite versions is this chocolate-scented playdough. It smells delicious and, because the recipe makes a fair amount, it can be packaged into little containers for a fun party favor or a Valentine's "treat."

Makes about 4 cups playdough

1½ cups all-purpose flour

1 cup salt

4 teaspoons cream of tartar

½ cup unsweetened cocoa powder

2 tablespoons vegetable oil

2 cups water

A few drops of glycerin to improve texture (optional)

1. In a medium saucepan, whisk together the flour, salt, cream of tartar, and cocoa powder. Add the vegetable oil, water, and glycerin, if using. Cook over medium heat, stirring constantly, until the dough has thickened and begins to form into a ball.

2. Remove the playdough from the saucepan and place onto a sheet of wax or parchment paper. Allow it to cool slightly, then knead until smooth.

3. Store the playdough in zip-top bags or airtight containers for up to 3 months.

CHICKEN TREATS

There are lots of reasons to keep backyard hens. They provide eggs, fertilizer, and pest control for your garden, plus they're definitely a source of entertainment. I don't raise chickens, so I'm by no means an expert, but I know people who do and have certainly been more than a little intrigued by the whole thing. One interesting tidbit I stumbled upon in some chicken-related research is that cayenne pepper is a great thing to add to their diet. It's said to boost egg production, help with circulation, and perhaps even prevent frostbite in winter. While you can easily just mix some cayenne in with the birds' feed, adding it to a homemade flock block—a big, hard brick of a chicken's favorite treats—is another great way to get it into their diet. And, interestingly, they can't taste the cayenne, so there's no need to worry about it being too spicy.

Makes two 8-inch treat cakes

2 cups scratch grains

1 cup rolled oats

1 cup cornmeal

¾ cup wheat germ

1 teaspoon cayenne pepper

½ cup crushed eggshells

½ cup raisins

4 large eggs with their shells, crushed

¾ cup molasses

½ cup coconut oil, melted

1. Preheat the oven to 400°F. Grease two 8-inch round or square cake pans.

2. Combine scratch grains, oats, cornmeal, wheat germ, cayenne, and crushed eggshells in a large bowl. Whisk to combine.

3. Add the raisins, crushed whole eggs, molasses, and coconut oil and stir until fully combined.

4. Pour the mixture into the prepared pans. Bake for 30 minutes, until the edges are browned and the middle is firm.

5. Cool completely, then serve to your chickens.

GARDEN PEST REPELLENT

I'm not a great gardener. I aspire to be a great gardener, and I put effort into gardening, but—alas—I am not great at it. Still, each and every year, bursting with optimism, I try again with the flowers and the vegetables. So when my plants become snacks for creepy crawlies, I do not appreciate it. Not. One. Bit. Dejected (and maybe even a little mad) as I may be, however, I never reach for synthetic pesticides. For one thing, they're pretty terrible for the environment and, for another, I don't want that stuff on the food I'm (theoretically) growing. Instead, I fight fire with fire . . . in the form of cayenne. A concoction of cayenne, garlic, and water becomes a spray that really does seem to keep many unwanted guests away. It makes sense, though, right? I mean, pepper spray keeps the bad guys away. Everyone knows *that*.

Makes about 1 quart

1 clove garlic

1 small onion peeled, roughly chopped

1 teaspoon cayenne pepper

4 cups plain water

1 tablespoon liquid dish soap

1. Puree garlic and onion in a blender or food processor. Transfer to a large bowl or jar and add cayenne and water. Set aside for 1 hour.

2. Strain the mixture through a fine-mesh sieve lined with cheesecloth, squeezing the cloth to extract as much liquid as possible. Discard the pulp. Transfer the liquid to a spray bottle or garden sprayer. Add the dish soap.

3. To use: Spray both the upper and lower surfaces of plants you want to protect.

SQUIRREL REPELLENT FOR BIRD FEEDERS 🌶

My daughter, who, at best, isn't interested in most animals and, in truth, is terrified of a large majority of them, is somehow extremely enamored of birds. She could sit and watch them all day. My kids can be running around, playing in the yard, and then, suddenly, I'll notice that she's become still and quiet as she stops to watch a bird. Something about the tiny, graceful creatures gives her a sense of calm, I guess. That, and she's too young for Hitchcock. In any case, we've put a few bird feeders around to encourage winged visitors to our yard. And it's been lovely, except for one thing: the squirrels. I mean no offense, squirrels, but y'all are straight-up mercenaries when it comes to getting food! Thieves, I tell you. Good thing there's the whole entire internet, because just a bit of online research led me to the easiest solution ever—one I wish I'd thought of myself. Cayenne! Turns out birds can't really taste it, but squirrels can—and they don't like it! So, keeping squirrels out of your birdseed is as easy as sprinkling it with cayenne. Problem solved.

Makes about 1 pound

1 pound wild birdseed

3 tablespoons cayenne pepper

1. Pour the birdseed into a large bowl or clean bucket. Add the cayenne to the birdseed mix and stir until the cayenne pepper is evenly distributed throughout the mixture.

2. Transfer the spicy birdseed to a large storage container with a lid. Store in a cool dry place. Give the container a shake to redistribute the cayenne pepper throughout the seed mixture before each use.

COCOA MULCH 101 🍫

Years ago, we lived in the garden apartment of a brownstone on a beautiful street in Brooklyn. We rented the place from the family upstairs, who kept the small area in front of the home beautifully landscaped. I have a distinct memory of walking outside one spring morning and being overcome with the over-whelming aroma of chocolate. I love New York City, but it's not exactly known for smelling great, so I was more than a little confused. And my confusion was compounded when I saw David, the owner, spreading around a bag of mulch, because I *hate* the smell of mulch. And then, weirder still, it became clear that the amazing smell of chocolate was coming from the mulch! My mind was blown. Cocoa bean mulch is a thing and it's amazing. If you're looking for an economical, all-natural, green product for your garden and yard and aren't familiar with cocoa mulch, here's the scoop:

Cocoa bean mulch is made from the shells that come off during the roasting process. They're often simply discarded during manufacturing. Putting them to use as a mulch makes this an environmentally friendly option.

Buying cocoa bean mulch is as easy as visiting your local garden shop. Most well-stocked nurseries and garden centers sell it. Cocoa mulch is a medium brown color when fresh but darkens with age. It looks great with just about any kind of planting. Even better, it suppresses weeds from growing, so you won't have to get into that annoying work as often.

And then there's that smell! When the mulch is fresh, it

really, truly smells like chocolate. Sadly, the fragrance fades, but for a few glorious weeks, you'll have that gorgeous aroma wafting through the air.

One word of warning: Cocoa mulch is toxic to dogs and cats for the same reason that chocolate is poisonous to them. So, if you have pets, you'll either have to skip the mulch or reserve it for use in areas where your pets can't get to it.

Note: If you believe your pet may have eaten cocoa hull mulch, take them to a veterinarian immediately.

DEER DETERRENT

Hostas grow like crazy in my yard. They're one of the most popular perennials around: they make a lovely border and, frankly, they're really hard to kill. Therefore, I love them. Want to know who else loves hostas? Deer! Unless I use some kind of voodoo to keep them away, the deer go to town on my hostas, treating my landscaping like a salad bar! But, as they say, an ounce of prevention—or, in this case 128 ounces of prevention—is worth a pound of cure. This cayenne-heavy, inexpensive, all-natural deer repellent is just that cure. Spray it on any plants you suspect the deer (or bunnies!) might like to chow down on and enjoy a summer of vibrant, beautiful foliage.

Makes about 1 gallon

3 large eggs

3 tablespoons milk

3 cloves garlic

3 tablespoons cayenne pepper

1 gallon warm water

1. Combine the eggs, milk, garlic, cayenne pepper, and 2 cups of water in a blender or food processor and puree.

2. Discard the pulp and transfer the liquid to a gallon-sized jug or other lidded container.

3. Add the remaining 14 cups of water and stir to combine.

4. Leave the mixture to steep at room temperature for 24 hours.

5. To use: Transfer the liquid to a spray bottle or garden sprayer. Spray plants all over with your homemade deer deterrent. Reapply periodically, especially after a rain.

ACKNOWLEDGMENTS

Sharon Bowers, agent extraordinaire, you must feel that your hand is super-glued to mine at this point, having shepherded me through two books amid a global pandemic (and then some!). Thank you for your patience, guidance, and unending support. Whew!

To Ann Triestman, thank you for yet another opportunity to contribute to the W. W. Norton/Countryman Press library. Six books in, and I still can't believe you're letting me do this. Thanks, too, to Isabel McCarthy and the rest of the amazing team at The Countryman Press for making me look so good.

Sarah Strong, thank you for your valiant recipe testing, attention to detail, and general enthusiasm.

To Gary Guittard, thank you for your generosity of time and your incredible insight into the history, craft, and business of chocolate. And to Charlotte Grant at the World Cocoa Foundation for giving me such an incredible education.

To my friends and family, including The Supper Club Mamas and the Havdahlings, who dutifully tasted, tested, and helped me tweak so many of the recipes and remedies in this book, I can't thank you enough. Special thanks to my mother-in-law, Bonnie Scherr; my mom, Harriet Isack; and my brother, Mike Isack, who are unfaltering cheerleaders and recipe testing machines.

Mads and Izz, just like cocoa and cayenne, you bring depth, fire, richness, sweetness, and joy to every single day. I am lucky to be your mama.

And, finally, to my Mitchell, for supporting every single one of my hairbrained ideas with love, patience, enthusiasm, humor, and corrected grammar. I love you.

CREDITS

Page 12: © massman / iStockphoto
.com

Page 15: © Almaje / iStockphoto.com

Page 16: © Mizina / iStockphoto.com

Page 18: © Lisovskaya / iStockphoto
.com

Page 23: © fcafotodigital / iStockphoto.
com

Page 25: © Piotr Marcinski /
iStockphoto.com

Page 31: © carlosgaw / iStockphoto
.com

Page 36: © VeselovaElena/ iStockphoto.
com

Page 38: © Alikaj2582 / iStockphoto
.com

Page 41: © Tatiana Volgutova /
iStockphoto.com

Page 47: © Montreal_Photos /
iStockphoto.com

Page 49: © skarau / iStockphoto.com

Page 52: © AnnaPustynnikova /
iStockphoto.com

Page 63: © MurzikNata / iStockphoto
.com

Page 64: © AlexPro9500 / iStockphoto.
com

Page 68: © bhofack2 / iStockphoto
.com

Page 83: © Tatiana Volgutova /
iStockphoto.com

Page 90: © bhofack2 / iStockphoto
.com

Page 94: © rudisill / iStockphoto.com

Page 102: © Nataly Hanin / iStockphoto.
com

Page 109: © Rimma_Bondarenko /
iStockphoto.com

Page 115: © Silberkorn / iStockphoto
.com

Page 117: © manyakotic / iStockphoto.
com

Page 121: © asab974 / iStockphoto
.com

Page 125: © AlexPro9500 / iStockphoto.
com

Page 127: © Pinkybird / iStockphoto
.com

Page 132: © JohnnyMad / iStockphoto
.com

Page 137: © hideous410photographer /
iStockphoto.com

Page 144: © bhofack2 / iStockphoto
.com

Page 147: © HandmadePictures /
iStockphoto.com

Page 151: © Bartosz Luczak /
iStockphoto.com

Page 153: © jenifoto / iStockphoto
.com

Page 160: © fotografiche / iStockphoto.
com

Page 164: © Foxys_forest_manufacture
/ iStockphoto.com

Page 167: © Pinkybird / iStockphoto
.com

Page 168: © OlgaMiltsova / iStockphoto.
com

Page 178: © themacx / iStockphoto
.com

Page 183: © al62 / iStockphoto.com

Page 184: © tacar / iStockphoto.com

Page 189: © V_ace / iStockphoto
.com

Page 195: © Seva_blsv / iStockphoto
.com

Page 202: © Svittlana / iStockphoto
.com

Page 205: © kazmulka / iStockphoto
.com

Page 211: © Sohadiszno / iStockphoto.
com

Page 213: © Sohadiszno / iStockphoto.
com

Page 215: © oykuozgu / iStockphoto
.com

Page 221: © yipengge / iStockphoto
.com

Page 228: © Reimphoto / iStockphoto.
com

Page 230: © nautiluz56 / iStockphoto.
com

Page 232: © benstevens / iStockphoto.
com

Page 237: © Annapuzatykh /
iStockphoto.com

Page 245: © 7823 / iStockphoto
.com

Page 247: © Charlotte Bleijenberg /
iStockphoto.com

INDEX